Copyright© 2015
Howard H. Irvin
Chicago, Illinois

ALL RIGHTS RESERVED
No part of this publication may be reproduced, transmitted, stored in an information retrieval system, or used in any form or by any means, graphic, electronic, mechical, photocopying, recording or otherwise without the prior written permission of the publisher.

ISBN-13: 978-1-939722-03-4
ISBN-10: 1939722039

Published by Technology Management Associates, Inc.
Mount Prospect, Illinois

People, Places and *Tough* /Plastics

The developer of Cycolac™ ABS takes you behind the scenes of his remarkable life and his work that made possible unbreakable Lego™ toys, telephone housings, and thousands of other products

Howard H. Irvin

TABLE OF CONTENTS

Dedication — i
About the Author — ii
About the Collaborator — iii
Advance Praise for this Book — iv
Acknowledgements — vii
Foreward — viii
Author's Note — ix

PART 1: EARLY LIFE
1. Destination: America — 13
2. Family Background — 16
3. First Luck — 21
4. Rose Poly — 24
5. Meeting Henry Ford — 29
6. Second Luck — 33

PART 2: PLASTICS, PLASTICS, TOUGH PLASTICS
7. Third Luck — 39
8. Hidden in Plain Sight — 41
9. Not Your Typical Resin — 44
10. From Small Beginnings — 49
11. People, People, People — 53
12. Business Schools — 60
13. A Point of View — 64
14. International Expansion — 67
15. Decision to Retire — 79

PART 3: LIFE BEYOND PLASTICS
16. Try, Try Again — 87
17. International Consulting — 90
18. A Taste for Art and Cheese — 100
19. Personal Observations on Europe — 103
20. Morocco, Egypt and Israel — 120

21.	South of the Border	127
22.	Chicago People	133
23.	Long-term Relationships	142

SOME PARTING THOUGHTS

24.	Decades, Distances, Discoveries	151

APPENDIX

China, 1974 — 162
Chapter Notes — 173

INDEX — 175

DEDICATION

I dedicate this book to Libby, my wife and "partner in crime" for 71 years and counting. What I have achieved could never have happened without Libby's support in my work and travels, and particularly in her judgment on important people that I had to hire. Thank you, Libby.

> The "partners in crime", Libby and Howard, passed away within ten months of each other. Libby died on March 31, 2016, and Howard joined her on February 1, 2017. They are now together on their final adventure and loving every minute of it!

ABOUT THE AUTHOR

Howard H. Irvin is a pioneer in the development of the Cycolac brand of ABS (acrylonitrile butadyrene styrene) at Borg-Warner Chemicals (originally known as Marbon); the groundbreaking plastic was first used in portable radio cabinets for RCA and most famously for AT&T's color telephones. Cycolac was the first moldable plastic that was not only hard and rigid, but also tough, not brittle like polystyrene.

As Vice President and Technical Director of the company, he oversaw about 50 degreed professionals and technicians at the company's laboratories in West Virginia. He retired in 1982 as Vice President of Borg-Warner Corporation after having been President of Borg-Warner International, with a half-dozen plants in North America, Europe and Asia.

He describes relationships and encounters with well-known individuals, including Henry Ford, Henry Kissinger, General Electric's Jack Welch and Borg-Warner's Jerry Dempsey and Jim Beré.

His corporate responsibilities included extensive travel in Europe and Asia. He offers colorful commentaries on his business and personal globe-trotting experiences.

He immigrated in 1938 to the United States from Munich just a few years before Hitler's onslaught against German Jews. Knowing very little English when he arrived, he resolved to work hard to succeed in his adopted country.

His post-retirement global consulting to the plastics industry spans 30+ years. He was awarded an honorary doctorate in May, 1987, from Rose-Hulman Institute of Technology, where he earned a Bachelor's Degree in Chemical Engineering with high honors from its predecessor, Rose Polytechnic Institute, in 1943. He joined Rose's Board of Trustees in 1976 and has Emeritus Trustee status.

He and his wife, the former Libby Tarler, celebrated their 70th wedding anniversary in September, 2013.

Visit Howard Irvin's website at www.howardirvin.com and see his YouTube video at http://youtu.be/VJNnwpj_pLA

ABOUT THE COLLABORATOR

Joanne F. Gucwa is a former food biochemist and a lifelong enthusiast of valid research, good writing and practical science. This latest cooperative venture with Howard Irvin continues the multi-decade string of technical projects they've shared. A graduate of Illinois Institute of Technology and Northwestern University's Kellogg Graduate School of Management, she has maintained her Certified Management Consultant status since 1982.

She established what is now Technology Management Associates, Inc. in 1973 (www.techmanage.com) and BioTech Circle in 2001 (www.techmanage.net). She is writing *BioFables*, a series of "stealth technology" adventure stories for children. She maintains several other websites, blogs on health and technology issues and actively participates in selected social media. An avid hiker, skier and traveler, she lives with her husband in a northwest suburb of Chicago.

ADVANCE PRAISE FOR THE BOOK

I was excited to read Howard's book, because I found there are many business related information worthy for us, but we did not know. The book is reader-friendly with plain words and sentences for non-native English speakers. It is a kind of non-fiction of modern business history.

He paid attention to establish good business relations beneficial for both sides (such as always leave information worthy to visiting companies). His business policy is so practical and valuable, those that we often pay less attention to in daily business lives.

Howard's thoughts are very useful for people now doing business, especially managers and/or high-level employees. The book may be worthy for middle and senior managers in companies.

His policies to employ No2. and No.3 people with reasons and no prima donnas are thoughtful suggestions for the present. In Japan, people who do not want to work more than what their job description says are said to be increasing.

Kazumi Iino, President, I. Techno. Office Inc., Tokyo, Japan

Just as easily and accurately titled "A Life Well-Lived," "People, Places, and Touch Plastics" is a highly entertaining and enlightening read, whether you're:
- wanting to reminisce about sitting in the porch rocker listening to Gramps;
- looking for an inside peek at global travel, food, and hotels;
- hunting for an example of how smart innovation, hard work, and committed effort can invent not only a product but a completely new industrial sector; and living proof of many of the leading maxims in innovation theory today, or
- seeking reaffirmation that the American dream is alive and well.

Howard has a "voice" all his own, and his engaging and forthright style will capture your attention and belief immediately. Be warned – soon, you'll find yourself wanting to retrace his travels, stay where he stayed, and see what he did.

Justin Townsley, President, StarAnchor Management Group, Inc.

A treasure trove not only of personal information but of how entrepreneurs and intrepreneurs (entrepreneurs working within a company) actually make a company grow rapidly within a valid market place...(he explains) the way of moving from concept to product to take advantage of different markets...describes the creation of product, expanding the product, and moving the product globally...(ideal for) people working in companies that have ideas about how to improve those companies, entrepreneurs and intrepreneurs (and) people wanting to sell their ideas to their companies.

Enjoyed it immensely...Exciting...enjoyed the personal touch of the book and how it fits his personality and capabilities.
Paul Tedesco, Author of "Common Sense in Project Management" and creator of advanced AI products.

I have known Howard for many years. We have had similar experiences traveling the world for our respective automotive/industrial manufacturers. I am grateful that Howard offered invaluable insights and sage advice when I started my own business. He is a true friend and colleague. I really enjoyed Howard's incredible life story.
David Koelliker, President, Austin Davis Industries, Inc.

On one level this is a fascinating biography of a young man who emigrated from Nazi Germany to the USA with $10 in his pocket, and through hard work, intelligence and creativity made it to the top of his profession... an enlightening account of the way in which the industry in which he worked dealt with the challenges and difficulties it faced, the inevitable internal politics, and the process of bringing new products to the market. Along the way there are vivid descriptions of countries visited and memorable friends and colleagues...a riveting account of a life well lived in exciting times.

(As a relative,) I wasn't aware of the circumstances of Howard's early life — he was amazingly courageous and focused, and I found the description of his boyhood and his early work on the farm in the USA very interesting...the account of his career in the plastics industry...also fascinating.

I admire the fact in what is notoriously a cut-throat world of competitive industry, Howard always maintained a strong personal code of ethics that was admirable, and he always gave credit to those who helped him and who earned his respect. He also didn't suffer fools gladly and that is an adirable trait, too.

Engaging, informative, fascinating biography of a self-made man.

Nina Curtis, Oxford, UK (Nina is the author's niece)

In his memoirs, Howard Irvin takes you on a fascinating journey from his roots in Nazi Germany and landing in America with ten dollars in his pocket all the way through his personal and career achievements, as an astute businessman and leader in the plastic industry.

(I admire) his ability to continuously search for creative ideas that may not have been tried before in his attempt to solve existing problems or challenges, his ability to cut through the complexities of a problem and go right to the heart of the issue at hand while at the same time reducing complex issues to their simplest denominator.

Inspiring...Truly an American success story.

Sue Urso, retired trainer in leadership development, process improvement, quality management, customer service for business and healthcare (Sue is the author's niece)

ACKNOWLEDGEMENTS

A Very Special Thanks from the collaborator to members of Howard's family who have offered unstintingly their support, multiple reviews of the emerging document and invaluable advice for this project: Tena Rosner, Susan Bergholz, Nina Curtis and Merle Kinzer. Their warmth, enthusiasm and encouragement for this project has been a wonderful inspiration. Tena, especially, generously reviewed the manuscript at several stages of its development; her painstaking editing and content suggestions are deeply appreciated. Much appreciation to Justin Townsley and Wallie Dayal for their contributions. All of you have helped beyond measure in improving the quality of this book. Responsibility for errors lie entirely with the collaborator.

Thanks also to David Roe for generously offering to scan the paper version of China, 1974, saving hours of retyping.

Photos are from the archives of Howard Irvin, the Rose-Hulman Institute of Technology, Borg-Warner and books by Paul Pinsky and Micky Nakayasu; Joanne Gucwa photographed current pictures of Howard Irvin, examples of Howard Irvin's artwork collection and several of the people appearing throughout the book. Chicago scene reproduced with permission of Ms. Wallie Dayal.

Maps: blank country outline maps are from geography.about.com. Joanne Gucwa designed the map shadings and annotations.

Rose Hulman quotes and photos reprinted with permission from Rose-Hulman Institute of Technology.

Cycolac™ is a trademark of Borg-Warner.

FOREWARD

"Howard, you should write a book."

"Interesting that you should mention that," Howard said to me in reply. "Lots of people have told me the same thing." This was in early March, 2013.

And that's how this book came to be, arising from more than 1 GB and 10 hours of recording over 20+ sessions. It's been a marvelous collaborative experience.

Some background: I met Howard in 1982 at the inaugural meeting of the Chicago High Tech Association in Chicago (eventually evolving into the Illinois Technology Association, after an interim incarnation as the Chicago Software Association).

We were the only two people sitting at a large round table, so we had plenty of opportunity to get acquainted. He told me that he had recently retired from Borg-Warner Chemicals and I mentioned that I was a former research chemist. Bingo! Instant rapport.

Even more coincidentally, he was just starting his post-retirement consulting practice, and I was beginning to broaden mine, as I had just received an MBA from Northwestern University the previous year.

In the intervening 31 years, Howard and I collaborated on quite a few research projects, mostly related to the plastics industry. I learned some great tips from him, many of which you will read in the last section of this book, "Some Parting Thoughts."

After his shared office location on North Michigan Avenue closed, he rented an office in my small consulting suite on North LaSalle Street in Chicago. Howard's proximity was a real plus. He listened carefully to my questions whenever I asked him about handling complex (complex to me, anyway) business issues. Invariably, his practical, down-to-earth suggestions cut through the clutter. Wonderful AHA! moments.

Howard, thank you for all your wise advice!

AUTHOR'S NOTE

This book tells of an American success story. It's my story, the story of a 19-year-old who arrives in the United States in October, 1938, with nearly nothing in his pocket – about $10 – and winds up helping to establish a worldwide market for new products.

Now, 75+ years after I first landed in New York, I wanted to give a glimpse into some of my business and global travel experiences and I hope that readers, young and not so young, will find it interesting and perhaps of some value.

This is not an autobiography, as it's impossible, of course, to cover more than just a tiny share of my life in these pages. Consider this book as something of a smorgasbord, a buffet of recollections in areas that made a distinct impression on me: school, working to develop new products for the plastics industry and building plants around the world, international travel and the fascinating people, arts and food I encountered along the way. At the beginning of each new chapter you'll find images of a few products made from ABS plastic and several pieces of art I've collected, along with buildings and, most importantly, people.

I tried to distill this wonderful journey into nuggets of lessons or advice in the last chapter. Like the rest of the book, it's a collection of basic truths I discovered or uncovered over many years.

This book would never have happened without the dedication and the technical and structural skills of Joanne Gucwa. It was a great experience working with her in putting this book together.

Happy reading!

Howard Irvin
Chicago, April 2014

Part 1
EARLY LIFE

Chapter 1
Destination: America

I was anxious to get the hell out of Germany.

It was simply a matter of time before it would be too late. My parents would emigrate eventually, but I was in too much of a hurry to wait. There were too many signs to ignore.

My mother, because she had gone to school in Switzerland, recommended that we emigrate to Switzerland as soon as possible. My mother was very intelligent and spoke several languages besides German, including French and Spanish.

My father, however, did not want to go to Switzerland. He had been an officer in the German army. Unlike my father, most German Jews thought that, with the expression of nationalism of being in the Germany army, the Nazis wouldn't touch them.

Believing otherwise, my father began looking around for other places we could go in order to leave Germany. At one point, he considered buying a chicken farm in Spain.

Fortunately, we didn't go to Spain. Franco took over Spain in July, 1936, shortly after my father's visit.

I did have the opportunity to go to Bodenbach in Czechoslovakia (now the Czech Republic). This was in the Sudeten area, which was mostly populated by Germans. Unlike going to America, one could take money out of Germany in order to go to school in Czechoslovakia. I was therefore able to go to a technical university in Bodenbach for one year. During that time I got some basic technical education. This knowledge certainly helped me later on.

I worked for a couple of years as an auto mechanic in Munich. In 1936 I went to London to look for a job as an auto mechanic, but had to return after two weeks — without a job.

My father intended to get an Australian visa for me through his banking relationships. His brother, my uncle, had emigrated to Australia to practice dentistry. Unfortunately, my father's brother died shortly after he and his wife and children arrived in Australia. It was a sudden, unexpected death.

My father had wanted me to become a dentist like his brother.

"I have no desire to get into a profession where I have to put my fingers into other people's mouths."

And that settled that. It was the last time we discussed my professional future as a dentist.

But I was still supposed to emigrate to Australia.

It was now 1937. I was waiting and waiting for my Australia visa. We had no indication when the Australia visa would come through.

I persuaded my father to take me to the American consulate in Stuttgart to apply for a visa to the United States.

Fortunately, our timing was good. I received an American visa about 2 months after our visit to Stuttgart. I was really excited. I would now be able to emigrate to America rather than to Australia.

I had read a lot of books about America, not just about cowboys and Indians. I had a very good impression about the country and the possibilities it offered for me. In Europe, America had the reputation as the land of opportunity, as a country where anyone could succeed. It also seemed to me that Americans enjoyed more liberal relationships between men and women and especially that teenagers had much more freedom. Besides, America was far enough away from Europe -- and from Hitler.

AT THE TIME I WAS PREPARING TO EMIGRATE to America, it was necessary to get an affidavit. The immigrant needed to show that he would not be dependent on the state to support himself. A prominent social worker in the Jewish community in Munich, Germany, Doctor Hans Lamm, immigrated to Kansas City in the United States in the mid-30s. He proved to be a very good friend. It was through Hans Lamm that I got an affidavit from a Jewish industrialist in Kansas City.

I also got an affidavit from Paul Selow, a relative on my mother's side. He worked for the War Department in San Francisco, making all of about $5,000 a year. I was invited to stay with him. Originally, my plans were that when I landed in New York I would go on to San Francisco, on another ship through the Panama Canal.

My parents brought me to Cologne, where I got on a plane to London, since I was going to go to America by ship from a British port.

The only money I could take with me to America was $10, the amount immigrants were allowed to bring into the United States.

* * * * *

A NOTE ABOUT THE PEOPLE WHO make apperances in this book. Both my business and social life brought me into contact with so many people that it is extremely hard to pick out a few names that I felt had the most influence on me. Therefore I profoundly apologize to those many individuals I've come in contact with who aren't mentioned in this book, but whom I cannot forget either.

Whenever I traveled anywhere in the world, I found local people who became my best friends. Unfortunately, at this writing, I find that about 90% of them have passed away. So, all I have of them are fond memories.

Chapter 2
Family Background

Many aspects of my early years influenced my later life: certainly a taste for food, art and travel, but, more importantly, respect for people from different backgrounds, a willingness to work hard and a spirit of adventure. Here is a brief review of my childhood in Germany.

I was born in Munich, Germany to Jewish parents on November 19, 1918. This was shortly after the end of World War I. We led a pretty comfortable life in the Schwabing area in the southern part of Munich. A lot of artists gathered in Schwabing, which is similar to the Soho area in New York City. It had a rather Bohemian atmosphere.

One of my earliest memories is from when I was 4 years old: my grandfather on my mother's side took me to the main train station. I was always excited about travel and trains. What a wonderful experience! My grandfather was a very nice man. He owned a small department store in Schwabing.

Another early memory is my first day of school. My mother took me to the grade school on my first day. Starting school seemed a pretty normal event to me. My parents brought me up to respect people, so I was not a spoiled brat. That is probably why even my first day of school was so unremarkable.

We lived in a fairly big apartment. The photo of our building, at left, was taken during a visit I made in 2014. Our apartment consisted of a large dining room, followed by what's called a *Herrenzimmer* in German. This is a "gentlemen's room" that was only used when my father played cards with his friends or when he smoked cigars.

We had two bedrooms and a smaller room for the maid. Our maid took care of the apartment and sometimes helped my mother cook, although my mother cooked most of our meals.

Our apartment was close to the large English garden. That garden probably covered 10 miles. My mother often took me on her bike into the English garden. We bicycled and walked many miles in that garden over the years.

I also remember a skating rink in the English garden, near what was called a Chinese tower. It was about a 15-minute walk from our apartment and I went skating there frequently. I especially enjoyed the hot dogs, which were, as I recall, absolutely delicious.

My mother was a very good cook. I remember often watching her as she prepared our meals. All my observations of her resulted in my becoming a reasonably good cook. My cooking skills also may have developed because I seem to have inherited good taste buds, particularly for seasoning. As a matter of fact, I still have my mother's recipe for apple pie which she wrote out for my wife.

My father was a traveling salesman so he was home maybe only 1 or 2 weeks each month. As a consequence, I grew up very close to my mother, but I was never very close to my father.

When I was eleven years old, I was given the choice of learning to play the piano or getting a bicycle. Much to my regret now, I decided to get a bicycle instead of learning to play the piano. It was a good decision at the time, though, as I was able to travel a lot around the country on my bicycle.

I rode my bicycle to visit my grandparents in Gröbenzell, about a half-hour by local train to the north of where we lived and spent the summer with them. My grandparents' house was very basic. They didn't even having indoor plumbing. We raised flowers, berries and vegetables.

The pine trees behind the house made a perfect setting for the books I read about American cowboys and Indians. A neighbor's boy and I spent many happy hours playing cowboys and Indians among those pine trees.

During the summer time, my mother took me on vacation to the Bavarian Alps, where we stayed at the priests' homes. The priests offered room and board to people at very good prices. We enjoyed very good service and friendship there. It was interesting to me that the mostly Catholic population in Munich was not very prejudiced and that's also how I was brought up by my parents. Due to the absence of prejudice I experienced growing up, the kind of religion a person belonged to didn't make much difference to me.

But it made a difference to some.

For example, I was the only Jew in class at gymnasium. One time when I did well in class, the teacher (who knew from my school registration that I was Jewish) gave me a prize. It was a postcard. The postcard's picture was the head of a particular Nazi. I think his name was Schlagpeter. He was killed and made famous by the Nazi party. What an impression this made on me. My teacher giving me, a Jew, a postcard with an image of a Nazi as a prize for doing well in class!

Not that we were especially religious. We went to Synagogue once a year during the high holy days in the fall. I went rather reluctantly because praying in church was not particularly interesting to me. I've always believed that simply moral and ethical behavior of an individual and one's dealings with others was more important than praying.

As far as I knew, my parents made no difference in their friendships with people, whether they were Jewish or Christian.

That reflected on me, because I had many friends of all kinds. Most of my friends were not Jews; they were just kids in the neighborhood.

Three generations: my father, his father and me, in East Prussia.

Three generations: my mother, her father and me, in Munich.

Me, all dressed up as a clown, during Mardi Gras in Munich.

My parents, all dressed up

I enjoyed skiing in Germany

Chapter 3
First Luck

Chamberlain was visiting Hitler when I landed in England about a week before the boat would leave the British port and take me to America.

Thanks to one of the Jewish bankers recommended to me, I was put up in Whitechapel, in London's East End. A lot of low income Jewish families who lived there really looked after me – I was just shy of my 20th birthday and the $10 in my pocket wouldn't have gone very far.

No one was entirely sure how Chamberlain's meeting with Hitler would come out. Just in case, gas masks were given out, and I helped dig trenches.

Chamberlain came back waving a white piece of paper. He promised the world that everything was going to be fine. I remember being amazed that the people in England were as optimistic as he was. As everybody knows now, Chamberlain's reputation soon went down the drain and he was replaced shortly thereafter.

About a week or so after waiting in London to go to America, I got on an American boat. I don't remember anything about the trip except that we departed from Southampton and we arrived on time in New York around the 28th of October of 1938.

Peter Selz was a friend that I had grown up with in Munich. Peter picked me up in New York and took me to his house. I stayed with him for a little over a week while I looked for a job. All I could find was a night job in a shoe factory for $7 a week.

It didn't take me very long to realize that nobody could survive in New York at $7 a week.

It turns out that Peter knew Ingrid Warburg (of the famous Warburg banking family). Ms. Warburg was the head of the International Student Service, the organization that helps students from abroad. Peter took me to visit her. She was a very fine lady and described a problem she was working on that she couldn't understand. This is what she told me.

A man named Bill Thalheimer owned one of the biggest department stores in Richmond, VA. He had bought a farm in Virginia that was a couple of hundred acres and wanted to bring German refugees there to his farm, to make farmers out of them.

However, there was a law in those days in the States that did not allow giving visas to anyone who had a job promised before he came to the United States. Does that make sense? Maybe someone in the State Department can explain that law, but I sure can't.

Ms. Warburg said that they didn't have enough young people to run the farm in Virginia. In particular, they urgently needed someone who could take care of and operate the technical equipment on the farm. I told her that I was quite sure I could do that, thanks to my previous experience working in some automobile repair shops in Munich. So, besides using my brains I had some possibilities to perhaps also work as a mechanic.

Ms. Warburg told me that if I would go for a year onto the farm in Virginia and work with the few young people who were there, she would guarantee that she would get me a scholarship at a technical university somewhere in the United States.

Such good fortune! Her promise would allow me to continue my education beyond the one year I had in Bodenbach, Czechoslovakia.

I LEFT NEW YORK AND, INSTEAD OF TRAVELING all the way to San Francisco to stay with Paul Selow, I went happily to Virginia. It was early November, 1938.

Not having to go back to school right away, I knew I could use the time in Virginia to better myself in English. I had promised myself that from day one that I reached the United States I would only speak English and not speak German any more.

I did succeed in speaking English without an accent—except for a few years when I had trouble with "Vs" and "Ws."

Life was good on the Virginia farm. The farm was located in Burkeville, about 60 miles from Richmond. There were about 15 or 16 of us. A lady who ran a sanatorium a few miles away from the farm introduced us to American cooking. She looked after us in a remarkable way that we never could have expected, I think, from anyone else.

The Jewish community in Richmond, Virginia, invited several of us on most weekends to spend the weekend in their homes. To have this prospect of a year in Virginia, and then possibly getting a scholarship to a technical college, was more than I ever could have expected.

In September, 1939, I received a telegram from Ms. Warburg. I was to go to Terre Haute, Indiana. I had gotten a 4-year scholarship to Rose Polytechnic Institute (now Rose-Hulman Institute of Technology). Of all the universities that she could have picked, it was my great fortune that she picked Rose Polytechnic Institute for me.

I had never heard of Terre Haute, Indiana, of course, nor of Rose Polytechnic Institute. But that didn't matter.

I packed my bag (one bag is all I had). It was mostly clothing that I brought with me from Germany. Except, I remember finally breaking down and buying a $1 Arrow shirt, made in America. I really appreciated that shirt. It had buttons all the way down the front, not just the 3 or 4 buttons that European shirts had, where you needed to pull the shirt over your head to put it on.

As it turns out, getting a 4-year scholarship to Rose Poly was the *first* of the three biggest pieces of luck that have come into my life.

Fifty-ninth
Annual Commencement

of the

Rose Polytechnic Institute

February Thirteenth
Nineteen Hundred Forty-three
Ten O'Clock
Rose Gymnasium

Chapter 4
Rose Poly

It took 17 hours (or maybe even more) to ride an overnight bus from Burkeville, Virginia, via Richmond, all the way to Terre Haute. The city is in the southern part of Indiana. I arrived in Terre Haute around 11 o'clock in the morning.

The college was on a multi-acre site right next to the highway that went to Indianapolis, about 80 miles away. I went into the main building, which was the only education building on the campus at that time.

Ms. Gilbert was the registrar. She was a wonderful woman. I asked where I could go to get something to eat. It turns out that there was no food service on campus. The school was not going to open for another 2-3 days. She suggested that I go back out to the highway and walk a few blocks east, where I would find a restaurant to get some lunch.

Walking about 200 feet in front of me was another fellow. He was going the same direction. I caught up with him and learned that that he had just come from Brooklyn, New York, by bus. Meanwhile, I had just come from Virginia by bus.

Arriving by bus was unusual at Rose Poly during that period. Most of the students came from either Indiana or Illinois. We became immediate friends. The fellow's name was Mike Percopo. I learned that he came from an Italian family and had lost his mother and father. How he ended up in Terre Haute, I have no idea.

Mike Percopo was a very good looking fellow. During our time at Rose Poly, we were great competitors in class. At graduation, there were only 14 chemical engineering graduates. I was number one and Mike was number two in the honors class that was graduating in chemical engineering.

We remained friends over many years until he regrettably passed away in January, 2003. More about him later.

LIFE IN TERRE HAUTE WAS VERY GOOD. I stayed in the school's dormitory the first year of my scholarship; the Jewish community in Terre Haute paid for my dormitory fees. A year later, we figured out that if I moved into a private residence it would be less expensive for the community. So I moved very happily into the home of a family in Terre Haute. They owned a grocery store. Now the generous Jewish community only had to pay $1 a day for my room and board. There were 2 beds in the room; Wally Van Kampana, the other fellow in the room, and I became good friends.

Nearly all the students at Rose Poly went home during the Thanksgiving holidays. It was too far to go visit my parents (who had since left Germany and were now living in Massachusetts) for just a few days. However, I was lucky enough to be invited to come home with some of my fellow students.

We were well-fed. The Jewish community invited me for meals quite often. One of the people in the community was about the same size as I was and he even handed down to me some of his suits. I was very proud of those very nice hand-made suits.

The Jewish community, especially the Bloomberg family, was very supportive with invitations in many other ways. The Bloombergs owned a very profitable insurance business. I spent most weekends on the little farm where they lived and helped Ben Bloomberg in the fields. I happily worked on those weekends, chopping tree branches, digging holes or whatever else that needed to be done. His wife liked to play chess; I learned to play chess, too, so I was able to keep her happy as well.

THERE IS SOMETHING ABOUT ROSE POLY that I felt from the start of being there until even now, that it was more like a family than just going to school there. It seems to be pretty much the same now, even though the student body has increased greatly. Everyone among the faculty and administrators was so dedicated to all the individual students, and I believe that had an impressive influence on all the graduates.

The school, now called Rose-Hulman Technical Institute, is still rated the number one undergraduate technical university in the country. According to the U.S. News and World Report, it has been able to maintain that position over the last 15 years. I can say that going to school when I did was like getting private tutoring from the heads of the department. At the time I was at Rose, there were only 400 students at the university. They were studying mechanical, electrical, civil and chemical engineering.

The student body at Rose was designed to be kept small. The chemical engineering class consisted of only 12 students, so it really did feel like you had private tutors as your teachers. The administrators, the teachers and the students were all male at the time I went there, although that has since changed, which I'll talk about later.

THERE WERE MANY STAFF PEOPLE I ADMIRED at Rose. One whom I met, probably in my sophomore or junior year, was a gentleman by the name of Jack Ragle. He had done much worthwhile administrative work at the institute. I particularly admired him, among my friends in Terre Haute, because of the kind of person he was. To me he was a typical Midwesterner, whom I felt were such outstanding contributors to our country. Jack Ragle is one of them.
Jack is a modern, modest, very successful midwestern businessman, with a wonderful family. He did so many kind things for people, including myself, that I will never forget. Here is just one of many examples: one time my flight was cancelled and I felt comfortable enough to call him from the airport to let him know that I was kind of stranded. He came to pick me up at the airport. After a few hours, we realized I wasn't going to get to Chicago by plane, so he helped to find a bus going to Chicago and saw me off.

At this writing, fortunately, he is still alive; he has been very successful in the agricultural products business and also operating a drug store.

I HAD NEVER SEEN A CAMPUS THAT SEEMED so efficient and dedicated. What I remember best is discussions with my chemistry teacher, Dr. Ralph Strong, in my freshman year. At the time I had thought about becoming a mechanical engineer. By the end of my freshman year, Dr. Strong convinced me that I should take chemical engineering instead. He said that chemical engineering was just coming into its own and it would offer me many more opportunities than mechanical engineering would.

All students took the same courses in the freshman year, so I didn't have to make up my mind on a major until the end of my freshman year. I did make up my mind, and decided to take chemical engineering, rather than mechanical engineering. My toughest year was sophomore year. You had to take calculus, geometry and several tough chemical engineering projects. In comparison, my junior and senior years were very much easier.

The only quarter that I did not do too well was the first one because I still had some English language problems. After the first quarter that language issue was resolved and I had pretty good grades thereafter.

When I reached the upper level in my studies, I was eligible to join the engineering society Tau Beta Pi. This was equivalent to the Phi Beta Kappa in non-engineering organizations. I became eligible in my junior year and the question came up of having a Jew in Tau Beta Pi. This was the only time that I encountered discrimination at Rose, that is, when it came to joining Tau Beta Pi. Jim Newlin was in my class; he became chairman of Tau Beta Pi at Rose that year and made it possible for me to be accepted at Tau Beta Pi. I will never forget his standing up for me.

Among other memories I have about my four years at Rose Poly is my friendship with the family of my classmate Fred Kolb. He came from an impressive family and they were wonderful people. His father was one of the first dozen officers of the Army Air Corps. He never spoke much about this, though.

Fred sort of adopted me, and his whole family was extremely kind to me. I did feel like they were my own family. I spent a lot of time at their home and with Fred, and I also spent a lot of time with Fred's sister and his younger brother. Fred gave me a ride in his Model A to school practically every day from my sophomore year on, when I lived in town and had no way of getting to school.

I joined ROTC (the Reserve Officers' Training Corps) at Rose, but couldn't join the armed forces because I did not yet get my citizenship and was considered to be "an enemy alien" by the United States government.

I did apply for U.S. citizenship as soon as I was able to, but it took a long time in those days. I was finally granted citizenship by a Federal judge in Hammond, Indiana, in 1945.

I graduated in February of 1943 with high honors: close to a 3.7 out of 4.0.

Chapter 5
Meeting Henry Ford

I think it was in my sophomore or junior year that one of my fellow students (whose name I just can't remember anymore) invited me to stay with his family in Detroit, Michigan. It was very nice in Detroit.

As it happened, my friend's father worked for Henry Ford, at the Ford Motor Corporation. Since it was the weekend, he asked me if I would like to meet Henry Ford. Of course, I had no problem with that. I was very interested in meeting Henry Ford.

All I knew about Henry Ford was that he dominated the automotive industry in this country. Also, I knew that he was a vicious anti-Semite. I wondered at the time whether I should bring up his anti-Semitism in our conversation, but then decided against it because I didn't want my friend's father to get into any trouble with his boss.

It happened that Henry Ford worked in his office on Saturday mornings, so my friend's father took me to meet him that Saturday. So off we drove to Henry Ford's office.

His office turned out to be kind of ragged and old-fashioned. Frankly speaking, Henry Ford made absolutely no impression on me either with his conversation or with his personal being. He seemed just an ordinary individual of no particular outstanding achievements.

The problem with Henry Ford is one that, in my way of thinking, is very hard to understand or to explain. He started out on a farm, with little education, but became aware of problems with transportation and started out in the fairly early days to work on the possibility of developing a more mobile device for moving people, enabling something like an automobile.

Henry Ford worked on each individual part with great precision. He went from model to model, naming them by starting at the beginning of the alphabet. He waited until he had designed the Model T, which he felt was good enough to commercialize. The Model T really was the first car that got any recognition. As a result, Ford Motor Company, founded by Henry Ford, controlled the industry at that time.

Henry Ford, however, constantly fought with his Board of Directors and finally decided to take the company private. Eventually, all of the Ford Motor Corporation was owned by Henry, his wife and his son, Edsel.

After launching the Model T, Henry Ford went further in his technical adventures by finding ways to increase the daily output of the cars. He did this by inventing the assembly line, while cutting working hours from nine to eight hours per day and increasing daily wages for the workers from $3.50 to $5.00 a day. These were done against the wishes of the existing board and that battle was what led Henry Ford to taking the company private.

Henry Ford sold a tremendous number of Model Ts. He had the market nearly 100% to himself. Then General Motors got into the business. Mr. Sloan and the two Dodge brothers made car models that gained the public's attention over time. As General Motors grew in sales, the Model T lost quite a bit of market share. It was the Model A, sponsored by Ford's son Edsel, that finally improved the market again for the Ford Motor Company. At the time of the Model A's introduction, the Ford Motor Company was down to about 60% of the market.

There were two other things which are hard to understand about a man who simply was a mechanical genius. On the social and ethical side, Henry Ford was a terrible and dangerous failure. He brought in his henchman named Bennett to look after the private lives of his workers. He didn't want them to drink or to smoke or gamble, which he himself had never done. He wanted all his workers completely dedicated to the company and, practically speaking, to have no private lives.

It was the Model A Ford which really saved the company. It was done by the undertaking of Edsel. Edsel Ford was a much more moderate man and individual with ethical and moral behavior, quite outstanding compared to that of his father. His father never gave him credit for all his contributions and Edsel died early—at the age of 49—largely, apparently, to the fact that he had to live with someone like his father who wanted to build him in his own image.

Despite his technical genius, the other side of Henry Ford that is hard to understand was his extreme anti-Semitism. No one knew where it came from. Through his Dearborn newspaper he constantly published vicious lies against Jews. And he made sure that his newspapers were distributed in all Ford dealerships around the country.

Eventually, Henry Ford was sued by a Jewish lawyer for his vicious anti- Semitic publishings. Henry Ford lost and made a formal apology, but nobody believes that he ever personally changed his mind. It is very hard for me to understand how two souls that are so different can live in one body. I simply can't understand it. I certainly saw Henry Ford, when I visited him, only as a great technical genius and at the same time as a vicious Jew-hater.

* * * * *

I have puzzled over the years about the fact that several of my most intimate friends happen to be Jews. These friendships are mostly due to the accidental circumstances that brought me in touch with them, rather than actively seeking out Jewish people.

This leads me to thinking further about Jews in general and their status in society. I can mostly talk about Jews in America, who are still a relatively small portion of the society, about 2.2 percent.

In terms of contributions, Jews have stood out in this country and in the world.

First of all, Jesus was Jewish. And he certainly made an impression on the world.

In the Middle Ages, philosophers like Spinoza stand out. In the U.S. in particular, there are many prominent people in influential positions, including Justice Frankfurter of the Supreme Court, who had built a tremendous reputation, mayors Koch and Bloomberg of New York, Rahm Emanuel of Chicago. Then there are great architects like Gehry, with his modern museum in Bilbao, Spain; all the important people in Hollywood and the movie industry, and Broadway musicals that have been predominantly in Jewish hands; Bloomingdales in the retail industry.

The greatest share of Nobel Prize winners worldwide (22%) have been awarded to Jews. Einstein, though born and educated in Europe, ended up as a U.S. citizen. There are outstanding law firms in all the major capitals in the U.S. who have predominantly Jewish professionals. Many Jewish university professors and medical doctors have gotten outstanding recognition for their achievements and contributions.

On the other hand, you have people like Bernie Madoff, who practically robbed not only his own fellow friends but Jewish institutions. A man like that, on the wrong side of the street, can never be explained to me.

I still do not understand—even now at my late age—how Hitler became so popular so quickly, how most of the population supported him. One reason might be that during the Weimar Republic, quite a few people did not have work and the economic situation in Germany had very much deteriorated. The results of the peace treaty after the First World War weren't of any help in keeping the Nazis or the communists out of government at that time.

What bothers me to this day is that the Jewish population, who suffered so horrendously under the Nazis, might have supported Hitler if he had not been so anti-Semitic. This might be because the German Jews, unlike the Polish Jews, were very nationalistic. I don't think anyone will find the answer to this question that I raise here.

Chapter 6
Second Luck

Meeting Libby was the *second* of the three biggest pieces of luck that have come into my life.

I went to work for Inland Steel in early 1943. The Bloombergs, whom I had been close to in Terre Haute, Indiana, had a daughter who had gone to Northwestern University in Evanston, Illinois. Hearing that I was going to Indiana Harbor to work for Inland Steel, the daughter told me that she had a friend living in Indiana Harbor who had been with her at the university. She gave me her friend's telephone number and told me that I should certainly call her up when I get to Indiana Harbor.

When I got to Indiana Harbor, I called the girl and we agreed to have lunch together. When it came to our planned meeting for lunch, the girl brought two other girlfriends as her reinforcements. Frankly, she and I didn't exactly hit it off well, although both the other girls were very nice. One of those girls was Libby Tarler. Libby was running a shoe store owned by her older brother. Her younger brother was in the Army in the Asian theater.

I was doing shift work in the metallurgical department at Inland Steel at the time. I went out to make sandwiches for the night shift usually, and often dropped by the shoe store where Libby was working. She was very nice and tried to fix me up with her girlfriends.

I finally asked her "What's wrong with you? Why don't you go out with me?" She finally did go out with me.

We hit it off, and 4 months later we were married.

It's now more than 70 years later. On September 16, 2013, we celebrated our 70th wedding anniversary!!

I believe our marriage has lasted this long because we never quarreled about money at any time. Libby has always been very much liked by anyone she ever met, even to this day. In our life together, I've never heard anyone say a derogatory word about Libby. And it's been a wonderful relationship.

I cannot say enough about Libby's support and help even in my work. She became known to many of our customers. They always welcomed Libby whenever she was traveling with me.

Libby has a particular knack for looking at people and being able to size them up. When I hired individuals I often brought her in on assessing them. I would say that the one or two important times when I think I made a hiring mistake, it was because I didn't follow her advice.

To me, Libby has three particular attributes in which she is outstanding. For one, she is an absolutely terrific saleswoman. She truly could sell refrigerators to the Eskimos.

Secondly, she has terrific taste when it comes to clothing. Many of her friends always asked her to come with them when they went out shopping to get something special to wear. Sometimes, when Libby went shopping for clothing and saw other people trying things on that weren't right for them, she would talk to them and tell them the clothing they were trying on wasn't flattering. Then she would help them pick something that would be more fashionable.

Thirdly, as I said before, Libby has an excellent sense for sizing up individuals. If you live in a high rise as we do, you might get into the elevator with her on the ground floor, and by the time we get up to the thirty-second floor where we live, she has your life's history.

WE HAVE TWO ADULT CHILDREN: a daughter, Merle, who is a retired speech pathologist and a son, Robert, who enjoys dabbling in real estate. We also have one grandson in California who is now 17 years old.

Family is very, very important to me. However, if I included their stories in any depth, this book would become twice as long. So instead, let me just give you brief, favorite memories of Merle and Robert.

Libby and I went to Mont Tremblant many years ago with Merle for about a week. Mont Tremblant is a very attractive ski resort in Quebec, north of Montreal. It is a beautiful area, not only in winter but also in the summer. Merle was three years old at the time. She had curly hair and Libby always dressed her very nicely.

There were a lot of interesting people around at Mont Tremblant. I fondly remember Merle going around to all the people who were sitting in the sun and introducing us to them. This was quite an experience for all the people involved. It was obvious that everybody who met her, liked her. Remarkably, Merle never spoke baby talk from the day she started talking, when she was around one year old.

Our son Robert is three years younger than his sister Merle. Robert always had some enterprises going for him. I remember one summer when he was going to Ohio University. He spent that particular summer in Kalamazoo, Michigan, selling Webster's Dictionary house- to-house. Robert was quite a salesman and was quite effective at it.

Another thing that sticks in my mind is also from when Robert was at Ohio University. He bought an old hearse for I think fifty dollars (or maybe even less). For a fee, he would transport many of the students at school. I guess they thought it was fun to ride in a hearse. Robert did this for, I believe, over a year before he sold the hearse, probably at a profit.

PART 2
PLASTICS, PLASTICS, TOUGH PLASTICS

Chapter 7
Third Luck

After graduation, I began looking for a job and soon found one with TRW.

However, when TRW found out I was Jewish, they withdrew the offer. In what was very common in chemical companies in those days, TRW discriminated against Jews; the discrimination was that they simply did not hire Jews.

I went to work in the metallurgical department at Inland Steel. Inland Steel owners were Jewish, so it was rather easy for me to get accepted for work there.

Prior to going to work for Inland Steel, I had the good fortune to talk to Robert Shattuck at Rose Poly. He was also a graduate of the school and was the General Manager of Marbon Corporation (a division of Chicago's Borg-Warner Corporation) in Gary, Indiana.

Bob Shattuck had asked the head of the chemical engineering department at Rose Poly to recommend someone to hire as a new engineer. The head of the department recommended me, so I talked to Bob Shattuck about the job.

The job paid two hundred dollars. Since I was planning to get married, two hundred dollars wasn't quite enough for two to live on. That's why I landed at Inland Steel instead.

After six months as a metallurgical inspector, I felt that Inland

Steel was overstaffed. You had to wait until somebody died before you could get a promotion. This was despite its being one of the more modern steel companies.

I decided to talk to the operations vice president and told him what I thought about my future at the company.

"The trouble with you youngsters is that you all want to start out as vice president."

"No, it didn't occur to me to start out as vice president. I just want a job where I had a good future to look forward to."

As a result of this conversation, he offered me a different job, this one in operations. I decided, though, that I really didn't want to stay in the steel industry. I wanted to look beyond the steel business.

I finally left Inland Steel and called Bob Shattuck. I asked him if he was still looking for an engineer. He responded "yes" and asked me to come the following Saturday morning to the Marbon office to discuss the possibility of my going to work for them.

It turns out that the office was previously a livery stable. It was located at 10th Avenue in Gary, Indiana. It sure didn't have the look you would expect for a chemical business.

After some discussion that Saturday morning, Shattuck again offered me a job at $200 a month. I told him I was getting married shortly and that $200 wasn't quite enough. Fortunately, he agreed to pay me $250 a month.

"But you won't get a raise for at least a year."

"That's fine with me."

So the following Monday I came to work at Marbon in Gary.

Meeting Bob Shattuck and getting to work at what was to become Borg-Warner Chemicals was the *third* of the three biggest pieces of luck that have come into my life.

Chapter 8
Hidden in Plain Sight

This small division that I came to work for was called Marbon Corporation. It had been started by George Borg, one of the organizers of Borg-Warner, jointly with a local mayor of Gary.

I didn't know anything about Marbon or Borg-Warner at that time. Borg-Warner bought Marbon in 1929 and had since spent another million dollars on it to develop products.

Marbon had started the development of a transparent polyvinyl chloride film. It was to be moisture and gas resistant, intended to be used as the outer packaging for cigarettes. The one thing that they did not realize was that without any oxidants or stabilizers this film would fall apart when exposed to sunlight.

Which it did.

George Borg looked to dispose of this investment of his. He was lucky enough to convince Borg-Warner that they should diversify into the chemical business. He then sold them Marbon Corporation for, I believe, about a million dollars.

Everybody at Marbon greeted me when I arrived. They were all very friendly. But nobody told me what I was expected to do.

In looking over the products and processes, I found that they didn't have any quality control tests for their cyclized rubber product. And cyclized rubber was their most important product!

Let me explain a little about cyclized natural rubber. This product required that rubber first had to be dissolved in creosote and then treated with catalysts. This process would make a rubber-compatible resin that would blend with the rubber and enable it to extrude smoothly into sheets or wire coating products.

The first thing I did was to develop a quality control test system. This system immediately improved the quality and consistency of the product. Then, within a few weeks, I got an assignment to replace natural rubber with some kind of synthetic rubber; natural rubber was no longer available because of the war effort.

SBR, the synthetic rubber that the government plants were producing looked like a good place to start. Their synthetic rubber was made with 80% butadiene and 20% styrene.

To develop the synthetic replacement for the cyclized natural rubber, I made copolymers of 20% butadiene and 80% styrene. These percentages were just the other way around from the current products. This synthetic rubber product was called Marbon S. It gradually took off as a substitute for the cyclized natural rubber and became our main product alongside our rubber-to-metal adhesives.

AFTER THE MISHAP WITH THE POLYVINYL FILM for cigarette packaging, we went to work on rubber-to-metal adhesives. This was a product line that Goodyear Chemical Company had started. Among the first assignments that I got when I joined Marbon in 1943 was to develop adhesives for bonding rubber to metal, primarily steel. A rubber-to-metal adhesive would make it possible to obtain adhesion without the extra step of copper plating the steel.

We were the first to come out with this development and were the only company offering an adhesive that didn't require prior copper plating to steel.

This rubber-to-metal adhesive was used on all tank treads and motor mounts on movable vehicles during the world war, and it was all made in the single plant in Gary, Indiana. Even though it was a relatively small business, it was very successful and profitable for the company.

Because of this unique product of the rubber-to-metal adhesive, I was given deferment to the draft. Borg-Warner's special rubber-to- metal adhesives skills that I helped develop were used for making products for the Armed Forces, so I stayed on at the company during the war years.

ONE PROBLEM THAT WE HAD TO CONSIDER AT THAT TIME was security of the facility. As I mentioned, the plant was located in an old livery stable at 10th Avenue. Since it was already very obscure, it was decided that the best thing was not to do anything to call attention to this plant and offices. We were so inconspicuous that the operations were able to remain at the building during the war and for some time afterwards. Who would suspect that advanced materials research would be going on in an old horse stable!

Chapter 9
Not Your Typical Resin

All of our cyclized natural rubber went into cable insulation during the war. After the war, however, we temporarily had no new business except in adhesives. Signal wire insulation completely disappeared from the product front. Our Marbon S went primarily into shoe soles and just to a minor extent into cable insulation.

Once the war was over, a big problem was to find products that would allow us to grow. We had manufactured a copolymer of mostly styrene that had relatively small amounts of acrylonitrile. We got a patent for this blend in the late 1940s and sold that resin to the Uniroyal division of U.S. Rubber in Warsaw, Indiana.

Uniroyal combined the styrene and acrylonitrile resin with smaller amounts of nitrile rubber. That process made it into a tough, hard and rigid plastic sheet that could be thermoformed or extruded, although it was too viscous to be injection molded.

"Now, wouldn't it be nice if we could make a resin similar to what Uniroyal has."

I believe it was Bob Shattuck who said that.

We went to work seeing whether we could make a resin that was as tough, hard and rigid as the U.S. Rubber product.

The problem with plastics in those mid 1940s was that the major polymer product was polystyrene. Many children's toys were made of polystyrene. The toys were so brittle that they broke—in many cases even before you could bring them home. Plastics certainly had a bad reputation back then.

To solve the brittleness problem, we went to work on making an elastomer in a rigid product that had similar properties to the Uniroyal product.

We succeeded in making both the rubber and the plastic portion of the elastomer. Not only did we accomplish making both these products at the same time, we also were able to use the same equipment for both of them. As a result, this process not only gave us a production advantage over Uniroyal, but we were also able to vary the product's properties better than Uniroyal was able to do.

Bob Shattuck decided not to get any patents on this product. A patent would disclose too well the product content, the properties and the process for making it, so we never filed patents on the basic product.

At Bob Shattuck's suggestion, we coined the name "Cycolac." This name might make people think it was just another cyclized rubber product.

Our public relations people thought Cycolac was a bad name, however. Common practice at the time was to stick to two syllables for product names, and Cycolac had three syllables. However, Bob Shattuck prevailed, and Cycolac™ it remained.

After years of working on and off on both on our adhesives product line and on our new plastic product, we began manufacturing Cycolac in a small plant in Gary, Indiana.

The small pilot plant cost us just $5,000 to build. A gentleman by the name of Sam Russell had come to see us to find out if we had any jobs for his company. The pilot plant was the one job we did have, because the big chemical construction businesses did not want to take on a project that was only $5,000.

But Sam Russell did. He had worked for one of the big chemical construction companies and left them to build his own firm. He was ready to take on any project that was offered to him.

Sam finished the $5,000 job in good time. This allowed us then to build a few-hundred-ton plant. As a result of our good relationship with him, Sam Russell ended up building plants for us in the U.S. and in Europe. His company probably made over $70 million out of that first $5,000 job.

Cycolac went on sale in 1956. At first we had a problem selling it because it was new and it was considered to be just another polystyrene. I quickly changed that by renaming the product ABS (acrylonitrile butadiene styrene). To this day. ABS plastics are important plastic raw materials in a wide variety of products.

WE HAD ONE PROBLEM THAT UNIROYAL ALSO HAD: our product couldn't be injection molded. This is because it didn't flow easily enough. We needed to do research on this, but we didn't have an injection molding machine in our laboratory. Fortunately, we were able to make arrangements with a customer of our resin in Chicago. He allowed us to try injection molding the resin in his plant.

A second problem was that we didn't have very much resin to work with. We could fill the customer's hearing aid mold only about half way, but we couldn't fill the mold completely. We decided to throw the half-way molded pieces into the customer's regrinder. What we found was that the stuff was so tough that it wouldn't grind up.

At the time we were experimenting with the regrinder, it so happened that some engineers were making moldable plastic radio cabinets at the customer. These engineers noticed that our material wouldn't grind up.

"We have to have that for our portable radio cabinets to keep them from breaking."

I remember working hard one Christmas weekend to make an ABS resin that would have higher flow qualities. The resin wound up to be less tough than the original product, but it was still about 10 times tougher than polystyrene. We finally got the flow high enough that we were able to mold the RCA radio cabinets. We called the product Cycolac T, the T standing for Tough. Cycolac T eventually became the standard for ABS plastic around the world.

RCA made a big to-do about how tough their portable radio cabinets were. Elephants stomped on the portable cabinets in their national advertising programs on television. Later, in 1954, RCA got Vaughn Monroe to sing about their cabinets. Thanks to those ads on TV, RCA's portable radio cabinets provided the first big consumption of our Cycolac ABS.

THE SMALL PLANT COULDN'T PRODUCE ENOUGH PRODUCT. We needed to build a larger plant.

Our original plan was to produce about 6 million pounds of ABS per year. After we got started, we decided to double the size to 12 million pounds. I made the point that we sold 100% of the plastic resin into the end product. In comparison, the synthetic shoe soles used only about 15% resin in the end product. So, I reasoned, it shouldn't be too difficult to sell 12 million pounds of Cycolac ABS.

When we decided to build that larger plant, we used a company that provided site location services. We wanted to find a site that would enable raw materials to be brought up by barge from the south to a location that was in the northeast quadrant of the country; the site also needed to be relatively closely located to our major customers. Bringing raw materials up from the south by barge was by far the cheapest way to bring those materials to the plant site.

We finally decided on a location in Parkersburg, West Virginia, because it met those criteria. The 200 acres or so that we wanted were situated on the Ohio River. We built the plant next to a DuPont plant that also made plastic resins.

AFTER A COUPLE OF YEARS, WE WERE USING both styrene and acrylonitrile in pretty large quantities. Bob Shattuck thought it might be wise for us to make our own raw materials.

Styrene is the product that starts with benzene and propylene to make ethyl benzene; subsequently the ethyl benzene is dehydrated to styrene monomer. We first bought ethyl benzene from Standard Oil and dehydrated it ourselves to styrene monomer. After a year or so we built a complete styrene plant in Louisiana as a joint venture with the U.S. subsidiary of the Belgian oil company Petrofina S.A.

The deal that I negotiated was this: both companies would bring their own raw materials to the plant and we would split the products 50-50. Our deal worked out extremely well for both parties. The Belgian subsidiary ran the plant for the first 5 years and we ran it subsequently for the next 5 years. Obviously, product could be brought up by barge directly to the Ohio River site where our plant was located in West Virginia. This plant near Geismar, Louisiana, is now one of the largest styrene monomer plants in the country.

We got started in 1957, but we had to shut down the plant for six months since we didn't have enough sales to keep it going.

Chapter 10
From Small Beginnings

The next big application for ABS came from AT&T.

When AT&T changed from Bakelite to color telephones, they had chosen acetate butyrate as the resin for making their telephone housings.

What AT&T shortly found out with their color telephones was that girls kissed their boyfriends goodnight when talking on the phone and children often smeared mustard on the colored acetate butyrate phone casing. Lipstick and mustard stains became a permanent part of those phone housings.

Our AT&T connection came about because Bob Shattuck had a friend at AT&T in Columbus, Ohio. Shattuck had sent his friend a sample of our product about a year before AT&T made the change to colors. That friend passed the ABS product on to Bell Labs.

AT&T tried making the telephone housings out of Cycolac ABS. The stains removed easily. Fortunately for us, AT&T was in a big hurry to change material to mold phone housings that wouldn't have a problem with stains.

At that time, Bell Labs had to approve all products that AT&T used. AT&T had not gotten any approval from Bell Labs to use our material. AT&T went to Bell Labs and asked them if there was anything wrong with Cycolac ABS. Bell Labs said they couldn't find anything wrong with it. So, for the first time ever, AT&T approved and decided to use a product without prior approval from Bell Laboratories.

Most of the AT&T telephone housings were made in the plant in Indianapolis, Indiana. Once they started using Cycolac, AT&T continued using it exclusively for the next 5 years. The other big resin producers couldn't match our product. During those 5 years of exclusive use of our product, AT&T did not have even a single failure of a telephone housing to report.

ONCE AT&T AND RCA BECAME SUCH MAJOR CUSTOMERS, we started the plant up again and then kept on expanding as fast as possible thereafter for several years. Demand for Cycolac grew not only in the United States, but overseas as well.

Cycolac T now became the standard for a moldable ABS resin. I felt it was important to have a worldwide marketing strategy: if we had a customer in the U.S. who had also molding plants overseas, we could guarantee that the customer would get the same properties in the Cycolac T resin wherever he bought it, anywhere in the world.

We made good progress in compounding the resin powder to produce colored pellets. Although the competition tried to get their customers to make their own colored pellets, we pretty much covered the market with our custom-colored pellets. Customers preferred buying our pellets rather than trying to make their own. After all, we knew the process. Mistakes would prove costly if the customers tried making their own pellets.

WE FOUND FAIRLY EARLY AFTER WE STARTED MARKETING our ABS that this product was very compatible with different materials. That's because of its chemistry of both polar and non-polar molecules: butadiene on the one side and acrylonitrile and styrene on the other. Most other plastics didn't have this advantage.

We discovered that ABS and polycarbonate were blendable in all kinds of proportions; different proportions produced different properties. For example, relatively small amounts of ABS kept polycarbonate from easily cracking. On the other hand, 50-50 blends of polycarbonate and ABS were extremely high in impact strength. Thanks to the compatibility of ABS with different materials, we were able to keep one man busy blending ABS for all different kinds of plastics.

I believe polycarbonate was the first class of resin to be blended with ABS. We were hampered by the fact that we did not know what type of polycarbonate would be best for such blends. Actually, Bayer in Germany took out a license for ABS/polycarbonate blends about two years before our patent expired; they were successful in putting together and marketing different blends of polycarbonate and ABS. For many years, PC/ABS blends exceeded Bayer's sales for straight polycarbonate.

IT'S VERY FORTUNATE THAT ABS IS COMPATIBLE with many other plastics, for instance with polyurethane, with nylon and with many other plastics. We couldn't possibly patent them all, as our Cycolac was compatible with so many other plastics. So I went to the Patent Department in Washington with a letter listing probably 30 or 35 blends of ABS with other plastics and filed it with the Patent Department. I did this so that other people couldn't get patents on the blends which we had filed.

I invented a new phenolic resin combination, which was among the patents that I received in various plastics developments related to ABS. This combination was an ingredient of an adhesive nitrile rubber bound to metal.

The new idea, which I thought was quite simple but novel, was to make the phenolic resin highly advanced in curing, to an undissolvable state, by combining sodium hydroxide with the OH on the phenol before it was combined with the formaldehyde.

To address the unavailability of the OH group on the benzene ring to cure to the undissolvable state, we coagulated the resin at an advanced stage with hydrochloric acid. This removed any OH remaining freely on the resin, and allowed us to take the resin, which was still dissolvable, and make it into an adhesive solution by dissolving it in methyl ethyl ketone. We licensed the patent because it was unique and was very effective. It is still being used today.

BEFORE RCA, THE PROBLEM WAS THAT THE AUTOMOTIVE INDUSTRY would only consider using our product in the little handle holds for the door locks of cars. It was the small molders in the country who took these kinds of orders because you needed many different colors, but in relatively small quantities.

These small molders were also among our first customers. They grew with us, just as Sam Russell did, as ABS eventually was adapted for more applications in the automotive industry.

Chapter 11
People, People, People

We developed our resin without any PhDs on our payroll.

We also accomplished things that everybody knew wasn't going to work. It's a good thing we were too dumb to know that whatever it was we were doing wasn't going to work. But, we did make things work. And we had a head start for least five years. Even big companies like Dow and Monsanto tried but could not match our products whatsoever.

In some cases, the people we hired were chemical engineering graduates. But some of them were just young people who worked as technicians. Their education wasn't a factor. We gave all of them a lot of responsibility in whatever they did.

As I already mentioned, Sam Russell built our pilot plant. His engineering company, Crawford and Russell, then built a plant for us in Parkersburg, West Virginia. The quality of his work brought Sam Russell a lot of business thereafter.

In late 1943, when I first started work at Marbon Chemical in Gary, Indiana, I worked for Bill Calvert, the research director. He was a very nice person who gave me a lot of leeway in what I was doing. He retired a few years later, and so coming from being in charge of the development, pilot planning and scale-up operations, I wound up running both the research and the development departments. We always worked very closely with the production department because they needed a lot of support. We also did the initial marketing. As a result of our marketing activity, we always knew what our customers needed and how to meet those needs.

I believe we were very fortunate in having the same team taking the development of the Cycolac ABS from the first laboratory developments all the way to the final marketing to our customers. In many chemical companies, all these responsibilities are split. That separation made our competitors much less effective than what we managed to do.

We also treated every work employee in the same way, from top management to production people to janitors. As a result, it never occurred to the workers to consider joining a union.

Borg-Warner Chemicals earned the reputation of having the best sales and marketing organization in the plastics industry in the United States. We did this by making sure that all the people that we sent out gave the kind of prompt and well qualified service that our customers were justified to expect. For instance, all our salespeople had experience working in the technology laboratory. This lab experience made them not only effective salesmen but also gave them a technical understanding of the product that they were selling.

All of our technical service people in the field had previously worked in the plastics converting industry, many of them as foremen. Because of their hands-on, practical experience, they understood not only the equipment and the materials that our customers were using, but they could easily, promptly and effectively communicate with the workers on the floor of our customers in the converting industry.

We also instituted visits to our customers. These visits were made not just by the various administrative executives in the company, but also by ordinary people on our production floor. This way all levels of workers could better understand what our customers expected from us. Both our customers and our workers very much appreciated this opportunity to communicate with each other.

In addition, we developed very close relationships with our

suppliers. At least once a year I visited the head offices of our most important suppliers, such as Monsanto and DuPont. DuPont had a plant next to ours in West Virginia, so I knew personally all the people who became directors of DuPont in Wilmington, Delaware. Sometime in their career they had all passed through DuPont's West Virginia plastics plant.

I also had very close relationships with the top management at Union Carbide, at Dow and at Monsanto. As it turns out, the man at Dow who had sold us our first truckload of styrene monomer founded and ran the Dow business in Europe for quite a few years. I was happy to be able to continue my relationship with him during that time.

In general I made it a point of visiting the presidents of the most important chemical and plastics companies around the world at least once a year. One reason was because everyone wanted to license our technology. These visits paid off handsomely, not only in what I knew about our suppliers, but also what I knew about our competitors. We had a department dedicated to collecting and keeping information on the strategy and plans of the competition. Very helpful in planning our own competitive strategies.

We had among our employees a man with some technical service background but who did not have an engineering degree. His name was Todd Holt. Todd became a masterful consultant to our customers when we opened plants in Europe. He was very much responsible for the success of our business in Europe and I believe he also spent some time in Japan.

WE HIRED ALL KINDS OF PEOPLE. One individual, Robert Multer, came from New York to our facility in West Virginia. He had gone to Yale's engineering school. He was smart, but he was also lazy. Lazy can be a good thing, though, sometimes, because Multer had a knack for finding easy solutions to sometimes difficult technical problems.

Multer's father was a congressman. I had the good fortune to visit his father in Washington, D.C. where I had the chance to taste the famous Senate Bean Soup.

Yes, the bean soup was very good.

Multer left us after a few years to run his family's wall tile business. He cut costs by automating it, and was quite successful at it. He wound up writing an article on the development of Cycolac ABS for a British technical journal. His article was incorrect, however, in many ways.

ANOTHER INDIVIDUAL WE HIRED was George Sakach. He was from Poland and we also hired him directly out of college. Sakach started out in the technical labs and then went into sales. When General Electric bought Borg-Warner Chemicals, he stayed with GE for quite a few years and wound up running their business in Europe.

GEORGE BARRY WAS ONE OF THE TOP graduates of West Virginia University in engineering. He came to me at Borg-Warner, I believe, right out of college. I appreciated George's advice and the way he handled assignments that I gave him. He turned out to be a very constructive part of our business.

George was quite an entrepreneur. He finally decided to leave and buy several plastic chemical plating supply service companies. These companies had been owned by Ford Motor Company but had not been consolidated by Ford. George was able to consolidate these companies into one company. It was located in Detroit, Michigan, and Gorge put me on his board. I met Clemens von Arnin on that board. He headed the German chemical specialty company for whom I ultimately consulted. George built a very good worldwide business. Unfortunately, he passed away much too early, despite it being after he had built his business.

AL KAUFMAN LIVED IN NEW JERSEY. I believe his father owned a telephone company. Before the Second World War, he had a small factory where he extruded plastic strips. These strips were used primarily to make belts.

Al, who had emigrated to the US from Germany, went off to war. He was inducted into the services, and because of his German background, he ended up in the OSS, the predecessor to the CIA. He eventually rose to the rank of General at OSS.

Al mentioned to me that for a time during the war he ran French intelligence service in North Africa. Ultimately he was assigned to George Patton as Patton's intelligence chief.

Al told me about his first meeting with Patton. This story shows Al's typical behavior and character. When Al showed up for the meeting, Al's uniform was so shlumpy that Patton told him to have a new uniform made overnight and to show up in his new uniform at 8 o'clock the next morning, with shoes properly polished. Al complied, which was typical of the way Al behaved.

I met Al when he got into the business of building extruders. Al no longer wanted to make belts after the war, but rather preferred to make the machinery itself. So Al got into the machinery business, very successfully. I met him when I was looking to buy a new extruder for Borg-Warner's compounding services. Al's equipment worked very well and the machinery was reasonably priced, besides.

Every time I visited Al at his plant in New Jersey, I got new stories about his war experiences. These stories were all fascinating to me because Al indeed was a very fascinating, smart and friendly guy. Al finally decided to sell his machinery business in New Jersey, but with rights to open a new plant overseas. This he did a few years later, about 80 or 90 miles north of Paris, France.

Al and I, being friends, saw each other once in awhile during those intervening years. Once his plant had opened in northern France, I visited him either by myself or with my wife. Typical of Al, he built a home next to the new plant. Actually, it wasn't really a home but more like a simple garage for him to live in. Next door, though, he built a $150,000 covered swimming pool so he could have his chance for relaxation. Other than that, Al never spent much money on himself. For example, he proudly displayed the $50 blazers that he bought at Sears Roebuck.

Ultimately, Al decided to retire. He sold his business and moved to Zermatt, Switzerland, where he had a great view of the Matterhorn. What he regretted most was that when he retired, he felt lost even up in the beautiful mountains; he missed his business. I frequently visited him at Zermatt and always enjoyed these visits both because of the views of the mountains and because of hearing Al's never-ending stories about the war.

Al made a lot of contributions to the state of Israel, particularly for defense. He was able to obtain an assignment as professor at the very famous Haifa Institute of Technology, located in Haifa, Israel. The last time I saw him at Zermatt (which was about 20 years ago), he said on my next visit he would tell me all about the things he did behind enemy lines in World War II. Unfortunately, 3 weeks before I was going to visit him and get all the behind-the-border war stories, he passed away.

THERE ARE A FEW PEOPLE OTHER PEOPLE WHO WORKED for us that I would like to talk about.

One is the new research director we finally hired: Robert Springborn. He came to us from Monsanto Chemical Company and stayed a few years. As a person, Springborn was very self-centered. He eventually left to buy a testing company in Connecticut. This testing company was well-known, but he decided to rename it Springborn Laboratories. He even named the street on which the Connecticut laboratory was located "Springborn Avenue." Says something about his self-centered importance.

Springborn set up branch offices of the testing laboratory in Hong Kong. This is where he primarily checked Chinese merchandise, textile merchandise that was exported to the west. He set up another branch office for Europe in Switzerland. I believe he set up this European branch primarily so that he could visit the Swiss office at company expense.

After Springborn left, we hired Jim Spainhour. Jim came from the Carolinas and remained technical director for the company for a long, long time. He contributed considerably to the progress we were making.

ROBERT SHATTUCK, WHO FIRST APPROACHED ME at Rose Polytechnic Institute, was a wonderful boss. He took no credit for any of the good things which we accomplished as a group. He always gave credit to the people who were actually responsible for the work and he set the environment in which we all could utilize our own capabilities to be successful. He had worked for DuPont in West Virginia. DuPont was very selective in their hiring. I think he learned a lot about how to communicate at DuPont.

To me, Bob Shattuck was the most wonderful person that I, even in my old age, would say I ever met in my entire life. He came from a very modest background in Indiana and had never met a Jew before. He was understandably worried about a Jew getting along with the rest of the people in the company, especially since the company he was trying to hire me for was part of Borg-Warner, and Borg-Warner itself had never hired a Jew before. However, Bob Shattuck was sure that, because of my getting on with the other students at Rose Poly, that my getting on with people at the company would not be a problem.

What most impressed me about Bob Shattuck—and still does—happened after the release of Japanese Americans who were illegally (to my mind, anyway) put into what was not too different from concentration camps during the Second World War. He brought five or six of the Japanese people from those camps on the West Coast to Gary, Indiana, to work in our plant.

Bob Shattuck did this against the fierce opposition of Foreign Legion leaders and other anti-Japanese people in Gary. He had taken a powerful step against the injustice that was going on. His decision demonstrated to me the ethical and moral depth of Bob Shattuck as a person. As I recall even after all these years, we had no problems whatsoever to integrate these fine Japanese Americans into the workforce at the plant. What an example of leadership that Bob Shattuck showed in our non-union workforce.

Our non-union plant operated in Gary, Indiana. Powerful unions of the unionized steel mills were located all around us. In the one or two elections that we had, the unions were defeated. I believe the reason was that we always treated our people properly and fairly at the company. Bob Shattuck and I also spent a lot of time in hiring the right people. That's what made the business go.

I don't believe that Borg-Warner top management ever appreciated what a wonderful environment Bob Shattuck provided for us. That environment resulted in our becoming as successful as we were.

Chapter 12
Business Schools

In early 1961, I was given the opportunity to go to one of the business schools in the United States for advanced management programs. Should I go to Stanford in California or to the Harvard Business School in Massachusetts? I finally decided to go to Harvard because I thought there would be more contact with attendees from overseas than there would be at Stanford.

I arrived at Harvard Business School in Massachusetts in the fall of 1961. I was able to meet quite a few people from overseas, as I had hoped. One whom I was particularly friendly with was a three-star general in the Air Force. Our backgrounds and thinking about life were totally different, but we became good friends and really listened to each other. One of the first times we talked, I told him that in some of his ideas, he was full of shit.

"That's wonderful to hear, because where I stand in the Air Force no one under me would ever allow himself to make that kind of remark to me."

The program consisted of many lectures and a great deal of reading, 5 or 6 books a week. However, the only book that I remember and will never forget is a small book with the title "How to Listen." It changed my behavior because I think I never really listened and had always interrupted people. That little book, which is now out of print, made it very apparent how important it is to listen to other people's opinions and not to be too concerned about one's own thinking. Of all the hundred or so books that we read during the six months program, that is the only book that I really remember and that I felt had a great deal of influence on me. I took back home some of the books that we had to read. I know that the general took none of the books with him. As it turns out, I never really looked again at the ones that I had brought home.

My overall experience from this program did not change me very much, except that I learned how to listen to people. Most of all, I enjoyed people with views that were different from those that I had. It was very worthwhile for me to be able to discuss the various areas of business life with them.

Among the professors, I was impressed with a few and unimpressed with a few others. Here are the names of the professors whom I remember. George Baker was the head of the program and I thought he was very well worth listening to. The other professors whom I still remember fondly were Milton Brown on marketing and Isidore Strauss on business history. Strauss showed us that really nothing much has happened in a thousand years of business history and he expressed his thoughts on that very well. Another professor, Renato Thierry, was Italian. His lectures on business administration were very informative. There were a couple of other professors who were more impressed with themselves, I thought, than in teaching us students.

ONE OF THE BIG PROBLEMS at the Harvard Business School, I think, is that too many of their professors spend their whole educational life at Harvard. That's what makes them somewhat inbred. I think in recent years Harvard has tried to change this somewhat, but I suspect that the practice of remaining at Harvard over a full career is still basically true.

The cost of the program in 1961 was, I think, five or six thousand dollars for six months. Today, I understand the program is in excess of fifty thousand dollars. I think the cost is just terrible, but that's what's happening in the price of education, especially advanced education.

When Mike Percopo got back to the U.S. after the war, he had the opportunity to go to graduate school under the Veterans Bill of Rights. Mike asked me whether he should go to the Harvard Business School for a degree, since he had this opportunity. I told him "absolutely," that it would be a big step forward.

OVER A COUPLE OF YEARS, I DID SOME LECTURING at several of the better-known business schools in France, including INSEAD, HEC Paris, ESSEC business school and the EDHEC Business School in Nice. This opportunity came about when I met a French professor who became a close personal friend of mine; he had arranged the lecture sessions for me. One of the sessions was sponsored by the city of Paris.

Mostly I talked to the classes about how we at Marbon, as a very small company, were just too dumb to know what would and wouldn't work and so we just tried things.

I was not very impressed with most of the business school programs or their students, who, surprisingly to me, mostly asked very stupid questions. The discussions were in English because my French wasn't that great. Overall, I was not impressed with French business schools.

The one business school that I got to know and admire most in the world is IMD in Lausanne, Switzerland. They have wonderful facilities. I went to IMD several times to attend some of their programs. There was broad participation from all over the world: people came from Japan, India, Scandinavia and many other locations.

I got to know the head of IMD pretty well. He was a Norwegian who has since retired. Surprisingly to me, the new head of IMD came from the Harvard Business School. It was surprising that IMD would hire someone from Harvard, since Harvard is very different from IMD. and I have had no contact with him.

IMD does not concentrate on giving MBAs, but instead focuses on special programs for various types of businesses. The school holds an annual 3 or 4 day conference that any U.S. graduate of IMD can attend. This conference covers not only very different business problems in group sessions, but has professors from all over the world. Faculty from different countries brings really worldwide views to the table. To me, this gives not only professors but also attendees a great annual outlook on business throughout the world. I recommend considering IMD for any program or at any time someone wants a wider view on the world's business climate.

I tried to figure out how to develop a joint program between IMD and Rose-Hulman, the two schools I have tremendous respect for. My efforts failed, however, because it turned out that IMD already had formed a relationship with MIT.

25th anniversary celebration of my Harvard class. Libby is in the front, second from left. I'm fifth from the right in the second row.

Chapter 13
A Point of View

In 1968, people at Borg-Warner headquarters in Chicago made the decision to bring more of the top management from the company's different divisions to relocate in Chicago. The first division they picked for this experiment was the chemical division. So, in the late 1960's, all our top management moved into the Chicago office of Borg-Warner.

When the economy hit the downturn in the early 70s, they sent everybody back to West Virginia—except me. I made the point that, because of so much overseas travel and my many dealings with both the corporate technical department and the law department, I should stay in Chicago.

And I did.

We had a technical department in Des Plaines, Illinois associated with the Borg-Warner executive office in Chicago. Each division was required to make an annual contribution to operating that technical center. No one was ever satisfied with the results that came out of the technical center. The division heads complained to president Jim Beré that they were not getting anything for their money. Neither were we.

I suggested to top management that we take an unusual step: hire maybe a dozen or so bright scientists; these were scientists who didn't have the temperament to work well together within a corporate environment but could work well independently. These scientists should be given perhaps a 3-year contract and the money to develop some of their own ideas that could be of value to any of the Borg-Warner divisions.

But this idea never came about. Ultimately the technical center was abandoned and I believe the building itself was torn down. I still think today that such a movement would have been a good way to operate the facility successfully, rather than continuing to just spend money on research that no one appreciated.

The trouble is that so few corporate managements want to take certain risks—which I think this certainly would have been—but as far as I know, almost no American manufacturing company, or maybe only one) has ever made such innovative assignments to bright people who only work well as individuals rather than as part of a corporate team.

*****

When I came to America, my English was good enough for me to have reasonable, simple conversations. As I had already indicated, I decided that from the day I put the foot on American soil I would only speak English.

However, my European English education did not provide something that is very valuable for your life: cuss words. I didn't know any English cuss words that were commonly used in the United States.

I found that it was very important to learn "son of a bitch" as a generally preferred cuss word (or phrase) in the American language. I never did and still do not quite understand why "son of a bitch" is a broadly used cuss word. People don't really pay any attention to whether it's addressed to men or women. I just used "son of a bitch" without knowing how to spell it at the time. But using it did help me in certain conversations.

MANY YEARS LATER, I WAS UPSET about a conversation I had with my wife Libby, and I said to her "go fuck yourself." This was not very appropriate, obviously, and she was very upset.

A few days later I talked with a family friend who both of us knew extremely well about this issue. He suggested that there's another way to express yourself: instead of saying "go fuck yourself," say "good for you."

I finally apologized to my wife and said "good for you." (I think I repeated "go fuck yourself" after I apologized.)

The "good for you" transversion eventually became a widely used expression at the Borg-Warner headquarters in Chicago. Most people, knowing what it REALLY meant, had a big laugh about it.

I WORKED HARD TO BECOME fully assimilated into my adopted country, America. That includes the way I sounded when I spoke; I wanted to speak as an American, to remove even a hint of an accent.

On the other hand, Henry Kissinger came to the United States about the same time as I did, but he never lost his German accent. Kissinger's brother, who was a little bit younger, also lives in the United States. Interestingly, Kissinger's brother speaks with no accent. So, I think it's likely that Henry Kissinger's accent is a little put on.

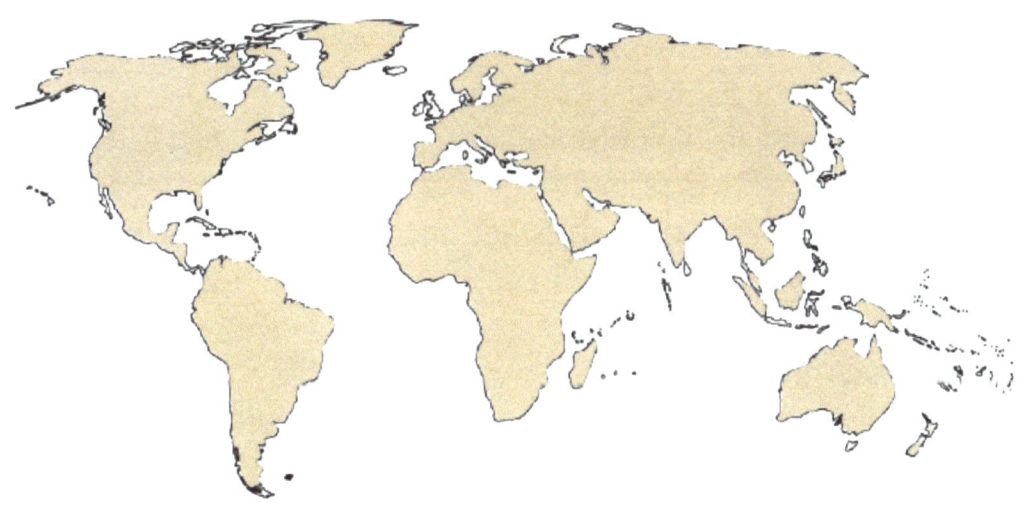

Chapter 14
International Expansion

The world was alerted when RCA and AT&T approved our Cycolac ABS material for their products. Now it was important for us to build up the manufacturing volume for Cycolac ABS in this country. With the help of Borg-Warner financing, we started spending money as fast as we could.

We finally were able to keep up supply with the demand in the USA.

"Bob, we should try to find a way to build our business internationally, given that it's going so well here."

"Why don't YOU do that?" Bob Shattuck replied to me.

So I set out to do just that.

UNITED KINGDOM. We found a company that had an idle Danbury piece of equipment to make color pallets for injection molding and extrusion. As it turned out, this company also happened to be the distributor of our rubber-to-metal bonding agents. We tried to convince them that we should set up a joint company in the U.K. for both compounding and marketing. After trying hard to convince them, they finally acknowledged that a joint venture would be of value to them.

About a year later we felt we were building up enough business and that it was time to produce Blendex resins in the U.K. We started looking for a proper location. Most of our business was in the Midlands, and so the question arose: Should we go south to the Midlands, or north to Scotland?

I was friendly with executives and members of the board of ICI (Imperial Chemical Industries of Britain, which was eventually taken over by Dutch firm Akzo Nobel in 2007). ICI was the first company we contacted. After talking to ICI in New York, we found that we had pretty good relations. However, we couldn't come to an agreement with ICI in the U.K. Why not? We had made the basic decision that unless we owned the majority of the joint venture we would not give our technology to any companies in which we owned less than 51%. ICI, at least in the U.K., was not willing to make that concession.

DURING MY WORLD TRAVEL, I had for many years visited the headquarters of Kureha Chemical Company in Tokyo on an annual basis and had formed a very good relationship with their research and marketing directors.

Kureha had perfected a Blendex-type ABS blending agent. The product used more butadiene than standard Cycolac and was more efficient than our product because it was much softer. Used in small proportions, it took the brittleness out of PVC mineral water bottles. Those bottles had become a big hit in those days in Europe.

Blends of ABS and PVC (polyvinyl chloride) were very advantageous applications for mineral water bottles. This application started originally in France. How do you make PVC crack resistant? Add a few percent of a modified ABS to it. In Europe the sales of mineral water bottles was much higher than in the United States and so the larger commercial market for ABS that could be blended with PVC was in Europe, most notably in France.

We needed to get the right combination of plastics to avoid breakage of PVC mineral water bottles. We put together an ABS product with a higher butadiene content. The blend was most efficient for getting higher impact resistance in PVC. In many instances the butadiene was from 5% to 15% of the modified ABS. We trademarked this form of ABS "Blendex."

Another fascinating application of ABS also came from France: motor vehicles. It turns out that military vehicles in North Africa had problems with pitting. Sand in North Africa is everywhere, and that sand pitted their metal bodies. ABS happens to be resistant to abrasion, so Renault in Paris clad their metal frames in slightly-corrugated Cycolac panels. These corrugated folds turned out to be useful in military, police and defense vehicles, as they all required extra strength. The ABS vehicle panels could be made in a range of different colors, including red, and our representative in France worked with Renault in the 1970s on building cars using Cycolac.

Since it was not at all economical to ship this Blendex resin to Europe, we looked for a way to build a plant in Europe proper.

IT WAS LOGICAL TO APPROACH KUREHA with the idea of building a plant in Europe on a 50-50 basis with Borg-Warner Chemicals. Finally they agreed to negotiate with us. Meanwhile, two other major chemical companies also wanted to form a manufacturing relationship with Kureha.

Kureha decided to negotiate with us rather than with either of the other two chemical companies that were interested in building the plant. Today, I still believe strongly that Kureha selected us because of the close relationship that I had formed with them on my visits over the years. Due to our already-long-lasting relationship, we were able to negotiate a 50-50 joint venture for less money than the amounts that the other companies had offered Kureha.

I went to the U.K. to talk to other companies in the chemical and petroleum industries about the potential location of the plant. These companies were both in the north and in the south of the U.K.

Although most of our business was in the Midlands, I found it preferable to work with the people in Scotland. It was much easier to come to an understanding with the Scottish people. They were also very much friendlier and tried very hard to help us. We ended up going to British Petroleum. BP was making both styrene and acrylonitrile in their chemical facilities. We acquired part of BP's property in Grangemouth, Scotland, to build our plant.

We assigned the building of the plant to Sam Russell's company. As I mentioned earlier, he had built our initial $5,000 pilot plant and reactor. He formed a company in the U.K. for the purpose of building our plant. He accomplished this very successfully, and with no overruns. We were very pleased because overruns are always a problem with chemical projects. The plant came on stream quite readily in early '63 and operated successfully from day one. We had exported our Blendex resin throughout Europe, and even brought some of it into the United States. It turned out to be a very successful business.

As we soon found out, relationships between management and labor and even pay practices were still in the Middle Ages in Scotland. Workers in U.K. plants at that time were all paid weekly, in cash. We decided we were not going to put up with that kind of nonsense. We arranged to have bank accounts set up at the Bank of Scotland for each of our employees. We then made sure they were all being paid by check once or twice a month. Because they now had a bank account, something most laborers in Scotland did not have, our workers enjoyed a more prestigious position in their community. The non-cash payment worked out very well ever since.

One problem we discovered: U.K. managers never tried to get a closer relationship with the workers. U.K. management never set foot in the plant to talk to the workers. The workers couldn't understand what it was all about when our American plant manager tried to start talking with them at the plant. As a result, the workers were all very suspicious during the first few months. Here in the U.S. this was simply a common practice for management and labor to communicate. It took the workers a couple of years to finally understand that there was no hidden agenda behind the plant manager being friendly with the workforce; eventually the workforce became very friendly to the company.

The next big question became where to build a plant next. We concluded that it would be Japan.

JAPAN. Bob Shattuck took it upon himself to make the initial contacts in Japan. After talking to all the major companies in Tokyo, he talked to the president of Ube Industries. The company was located in Ube City, Yamaguchi Prefecture, close to the border of Japan's southern island, Kyushu.

Ube is located in what used to be the coal mining district. Over time the coal industry became very, very competitive—and very unprofitable. Mr. Kenichi Nakayasu, the president of the company, was assigned to find other areas in the chemical industry to grow the company and to get out of coal. This took several years during a very rough period.

Mr. Nakayasu built the largest cement mill in Japan and he built probably one of the largest nylon resin manufacturers in Japan, among other specialty products. Although Ube has an office in Tokyo, their main headquarters are actually in Ube City. And Ube City is really a chemical town, an Ube Chemical town.

AS PEOPLE WELL KNOW, JAPANESE ARE very enthusiastic golfers. Mr. Nakayasu became a golfer when he was 60 years old, at the time he became president of the company. His late start to golf is because his predecessor was unusual and didn't believe in golfing as an important pastime. Once he took up golf, Mr. Nakayasu built a golf course about 20 or 30 miles from Ube City. This was up in the hills. And the government built a 4-lane highway from Ube City to the golf course.

He built a second golf course a few years later along with a hotel, also at the golf course. Every time we went to Ube City in Japan we stayed at this country hotel. It was very, very nice and accommodating to Ube customers. Ube also had the good fortune to get silent members to pay fees each year to the Ube golf courses. This allowed them to play any time they wanted, but in reality very few ever did.

The last time I saw Mr. Nakayasu (who was a big Cuban cigar smoker), he told me he built a third golf course for the older members. Since the country side there is very hilly, I told him that if he built a golf course he should have also built an escalator for it so that the older members could get up and down the hill. We then turned a corner, and what did I see? A big rubber belt that moved up the hills and down the other side to accommodate these older customers.

AS IT TURNED OUT, OUR RELATIONSHIP with Ube was extremely compatible. We maintained and continued warm relationships between all their management and ours. Our domestic headquarters at Borg-Warner could never understand the good relationships we had with Ube. We called the company Ube Cycon. Interestingly, other Borg-Warner divisions that had also tried ventures in Japan were never very friendly and further, they were never very profitable. We told them that the first thing is not to mistrust your partners because joint ventures are like a wedding: if you don't trust your partner before the beginning of the formal relationship, you never will in the future.

Bob Shattuck initially negotiated the joint venture with Mr. Nakayasu, the president at that time. When it came to working out the engineering and to working out details of the plant, he turned that over to me.

I HAD GONE TO JAPAN IN THE MID-1940s with all kinds of advice from people here in the U.S. as to what to expect. But unless I know a person and his views extremely well, I always try to make my own conclusions as I travel.

The one conclusion I made even before I left for Japan was not to follow the advice I was given: that you have to visit at least twice or so for the Japanese to feel comfortable to negotiate with you. I said that I don't have time for that kind of nonsense. What I did, going to Japan, is that I always had dinner with the people that I would negotiate with the next day. After one or two drinks, it was much easier for them to relax and negotiate and then we would just confirm the next day what we agreed on the night before over dinner and drinks.

Here is the way we conducted business negotiations in Japan. Our side made notes in English during the negotiations. Overnight, the Japanese office girls translated the notes into Japanese for their bosses and then back into English; the following day we would look over the new English version, usually made only minor changes in that version, and continued on from that point.

This process worked out extremely well for us and was in contrast to what most Americans always told me, namely that they don't trust the Japanese. What these people don't realize is when the Japanese say "yes" they mean:

"Yes, I heard what you said."

But this "yes" doesn't necessarily mean "yes, I agree with you."

This is one of the big failures and misunderstandings by the Americans I met who felt so negatively about Japan.

We developed fond relationships with the family of our joint venture partner. Mr. Tawarada had become president of Ube, and the Tawaradas took us through virtually all of Japan. We probably have seen much more of Japan than most native Japanese see in their lifetime. We went to the main island, to the northern island of Hokkaido, to the southern island of Kyushu. Everywhere we went in Japan we found some very, very fascinating sights. We were very fortunate that the Tawaradas took us to these places, because you weren't able to read many signs if you didn't know Japanese; outside of Tokyo practically nobody spoke English at that time.

THE OTHER THING ABOUT JAPAN I'd like to talk about is the new American embassy. It was built while our Borg-Warner ex-chairman, Bob Ingersoll, was there as ambassador. It looks like a factory. I told Bob what I thought about the building and told him that the first impression that foreigners get of a country is the embassy they build. His excuse for building a factory rather than a career embassy is that they didn't have the money.

This doesn't speak very highly of the decisions that are made in the State Department.

I did find at the embassy a scientific officer, an American of unusually great understanding, not only of the Japanese, but also how to behave as a State Department representative. He not only spoke Japanese, but even had a Japanese typewriter, which was quite a remarkable machine. He told me several times how ineffective State Department representatives overseas often are. He finally was moved to London in the U.K. Libby and I kept our friendship with him and his wife for a long time after he retired. He was one of the rare impressive American representatives I met abroad, among the many embassy employees that I encountered through the years. Unfortunately, I don't recall his name.

NETHERLANDS. When the U.K. did not come into the common market, we decided that it was probably necessary to build a plant on the continent. After talking to people we knew in Brussels who had chemical stabilizer manufacturing bases there, we found that whatever land that was available was too small for us to build a plant.

We went up to look at Scotland and at both Rotterdam and Amsterdam in the Netherlands. After looking at both sites in the Netherlands, and based on the promises made by the mayors of both cities, we decided to build a plant at a new location to the west of Amsterdam. We relied on all the concessions that the mayor of Amsterdam had made to us.

As it turned out, though, the mayor had lied to me and made promises that he never intended to keep. I have forgotten the specific details, but I've not forgotten the fact that the promises made weren't kept.

After we started building the plant, again for which we gave responsibility to Sam Russell, we found that there were not many plants in the Amsterdam area requiring three 8-hour shifts. We were quite surprised at how extremely difficult it was to hire a workforce in Amsterdam that was willing to work 8-hour shifts.

What else we found in Amsterdam that was unbelievable (to me at least) was that we had the biggest housekeeping problems in the Netherlands compared with any of our other plants. As you go through the small towns of the Netherlands and look through the curtains into the living room, you see that they are all very neat and very clean. I couldn't understand the glaring difference between home and work area.

We also had an explosion in Amsterdam. We think the explosion was caused by the rough steel spurs on the fire department's shoes when they were called in to take care of leaking butadiene. It's likely that the spurs created the spark that set off the explosion.

Over all, Amsterdam became our least desirable manufacturing facility. I have to add though, that Dutch people and the people in the area outside of work were very nice. And our Dutch executives were very efficient.

There were two things, however, about the Dutch that I'd like to mention: 1) they probably drank 8 or 9 cups of coffee a day during working hours, and 2) when it came to driving, they were crazy drivers who didn't care if they bumped into another car. It didn't matter whether they had the right of way or not. Worst drivers that I experienced anywhere.

BELGIUM. Tom Farmer became president of Borg-Warner Chemicals after having been stationed for several years in Brussels. He thought it would be better to move our European headquarters from Amsterdam to Brussels and asked me to set up offices there.

I wound up commuting between Brussels and Chicago for nearly four years. Brussels was very good as a business location; you could be in Paris or Amsterdam or northern Germany in just a few hours.

Tom Farmer came from one of the oil companies and to me was a good boss, as well. He let us operate unencumbered as much as possible.

The big thing that Tom Farmer did for me was to nominate me to go to China in 1974 when Bob Ingersoll, the chairman of Borg-Warner had been appointed, after being Ambassador to Japan, to Undersecretary of State under Henry Kissinger.

While Kissinger traveled throughout the world, Bob Ingersoll was managing the State Department in Washington. I believe it was because of Ingersoll's position that Borg-Warner got an invitation from the Chinese government shortly after Nixon went there to open relationships between China and the United States. We got an invitation to go to the Canton Fair in 1974, where we were among the first Westerners ever to enter the country. My reports of our experiences on the trip to China are in a later chapter. They were written in 1974.

CANADA. Next, we bought some land for compounding faciities at Cobourg on Lake Ontario; we ran that business effectively for a number of years.

After that successful Canadian operation, a thought occurred to me: wouldn't it be practical to set up a joint venture with a company that not only uses plastics but is also a producer of products in which they would use our resin?

As it turned out, the people who were selling our resin in Australia were the biggest vinyl pipe manufacturer in Australia. The company's name was Nylex. I thought that, well, they were far enough away so we can run an experiment there. Let's see whether a joint venture between a resin manufacturer and a converter of resin would come up with some new business ideas.

AUSTRALIA. We did build the Australian plant. It was located in Melbourne.

Regrettably, in board meetings we talked more about improving pencil purchases than about ideas for making new products based on our resin. This was rather disappointing to me, but fortunately it didn't have much impact on the bottom line.

Our main reason for building the Australian plant was to find out whether an association between a raw material supplier and a fabricator could come up with new ideas on fabricating new products. Unfortunately this synergy never happened, so we decided to sell the Australian plant to Nylex. When we did, president Jerry Dempsey and I both went to Australia to negotiate the deal.

During the negotiations, Dempsey was trying to get as much money out of the deal as possible. I finally convinced him that we also had to think about the fact that whoever represented Nylex would have to come up with a deal which would be considered to be fair by his own board. And so, we made sure that both Borg-Warner and Nylex came out with a result that would be just as fair to one party as to the other. That was the final outcome of the Australian venture.

BRAZIL. I visited South America only once; it was in the 1970s. At Borg-Warner we were investigating setting up a manufacturing facility for our plastic resins in Brazil.

The main purpose of my visit was to negotiate with one of the Brazilian oil companies to see whether we could set up a joint venture to make ABS Cycolac resins.

I believe we went to Sao Paulo to meet with some of the Brazilian oil company executives. After all the negotiations, though, we decided that the volume of business wasn't really large enough to put up a plant. As a matter of fact, we since found out that a local Brazilian engineering firm was contemplating putting up a small ABS facility.

Surprisingly, I was able to understand my Brazilian counterpart because he was able to speak Portuguese slowly enough for me to follow the discussion.

* * * * *

A story probably worth telling is the difference in services one gets nowadays from the airlines vs. what was possible in the 1970s.

I was on one of my frequent trips to Europe. We lived in Parkersburg, West Virginia, at the time. During that period I usually stopped for a day or two in New York for some business meetings and then flew on from New York to Europe.

On one of those occasions when I was in New York, I realized that I had forgotten to take my passport with me. Unfortunately, my wife was also traveling at the time so there was no one at our house in West Virginia. Luckily, one of the fellows who worked for me always had a key to our house. I called him and arranged for him to take the passport to the Parkersburg airport where a Borg-Warner company plane was stationed with 2 pilots. I called the pilots and told them to take the passport to TWA airlines in Columbus, Ohio, and have pilots on the flight from Columbus to La Guardia, New York, take my passport to where I would be waiting for their arrival at La Guardia.

Sure enough, the pilots brought my passport to TWA in New York where I was waiting to pick it up. I went from there to Kennedy International and caught my flight to Europe on TWA. These days, I think no one should expect that kind of service from an international airline on behalf of a passenger.

Chapter 15
Decision to Retire

When I first joined Marbon Chemical's research department, Bill Calvert, the research director seemed to me to be a very fine gentleman. He had come to the company from Goodyear Tire Company. I think he didn't have a doctor's degree, and that may be why he decided to use an outside patent attorney (whose name I no longer remember).

When it came to filing patents for work that was done by our research director and myself, the patent attorney always favored the research director to become the owner of the patent, overlooking all the contributions that I had made. This made me very unhappy, although I cannot hold our patent director responsible. To me, this outside patent attorney behaved in a very unethical manner and far as I am still concerned, he deserved to be disbarred.

When our research director retired, one of my first acts was to fire that bastard and replace him with an ethical-behaving attorney who filed patent applications properly. Ultimately, we ended up with an internal patent attorney at Borg-Warner, Bill McCurry, who became very close to us and was very valuable in all the patent matters that we had to deal with.

ALTHOUGH BORG-WARNER brought Shattuck to Chicago in 1967 or

so to become an executive vice president, they never made him president of Borg-Warner. I think this exclusion was because Shattuck always told management not what they wanted to hear, but rather what the facts were. He finally, sadly, retired early.

I believe that Shattuck's straightforwardness and honesty, when he became Executive Vice President of Borg-Warner, cost him the job of being the head of the company. He told those—well, the only word that comes to mind—jerks in the hierarchy the facts of Borg-Warner which they didn't want to hear. That to me is another sad reflection of the might and the capability of Borg-Warner's president and chairman at that time, as he was in charge of these decisions. Shattuck should have been elected to be president of the company.

WHEN I CAME TO WORK IN THE CORPORATE office in 1968, I gave up the chemical division where I had started twenty-five years earlier in 1943. My focus was now to help the other divisions of Borg-Warner to diversify.

Unfortunately, with the exception of the chemical division, these other divisions were no risk takers. I tried, but was really unsuccessful in getting any of them to give me help in diversifying into other areas.

The one exception was the manager of the Byron Jackson Pump division. He had been an FBI agent and then was a long-time assistant to the president. Ultimately he took over the Byron Jackson Pump division. He always lent me his ear and tried to take advantage of some of the opportunities that I brought to him.

In the meantime I kept the responsibility for Borg-Warner Chemicals research laboratories. Through a private contact I met Tom Kaiser, a biochemistry professor at the University of Chicago. Besides socializing with him now and then, we also talked technology. He told me that he thought he had worked out a process to make Vitamin D3 in several fewer steps than the current technology allowed.

I felt that this was an interesting opportunity, so we hired Tom Kaiser as a consultant. He told us that he thought it would take a research team about 1½ to 2 years to perfect his process.

The reason for reducing the number of steps in any given process is that each step produces lower than 100% yield; therefore, with Kaiser's new process the production efficiency would go way up. I assigned Jim Spainhour to bring together a small group of chemical PhDs to work under Kaiser's supervision. Remarkably, instead of taking a year and a half or more, the researchers perfected the process within half the time he originally estimated.

I needed to assign a person to look for opportunities to commercialize Kaiser's Vitamin D process. Finally we got the opportunity with Abbott Laboratories to build a plant. The plan was that we would furnish the technology and Abbott would furnish the funds required to build the plant. Abbott was interested in the project because they were going to use the Vitamin D3 in baby products.

A few days before the final discussions with Abbott, I went to the top people at Borg-Warner's management, which included Jim Beré and several other vice presidents in Chicago. By this time, Bob Shattuck had already retired.

I told management of the final arrangements we developed at Abbott before the final signing with them. I believe this was just before the 4th of July weekend. I told them of the opportunities we had.

Jim Beré said: "The policy of Borg-Warner is never to get into products that end up in the human body."

That was the first time that I had heard of this so-called policy. Beré invented it right at this meeting.

There was no reason why Beré had to invent this particular policy at that particular meeting. Every month we had carefully advised top management at Borg-Warner of what we were doing in developing this new process of Vitamin D3.

I later learned that Beré was a director of Abbott, and Abbott at that time had some difficult problems with their product testing procedures and was in quite some trouble.

Borg-Warner could have developed into one of the largest chemical companies world wide, with Vitamin D3 being the first in a line of pharmaceutical products. The opportunity was extraordinary. We had a team of young PhD researchers working on improving the Vitamin D3 production process, they accomplished their goal in far less time than even Tom Kaiser anticipated, and the approximately $1 million investment would have been a really inexpensive way to get into the pharmaceutical business.

This was another reason that embittered me about working for Beré as the top executive of the company.

As I mentioned earlier, I made a point that every time I went overseas I met with top people in major chemical companies; I did this at least once a year. I didn't want to waste anyone's time with meaningless visits, however. To make sure that my visits were welcome, I always left some information with the people I visited that could be of value to them; my hope was to get some information of value from them in return.

As part of this process I developed a real friendship with Dr. Herbert Willersinn. He was one of the chemists that was running the acrylic latex laboratories for BASF, a large European chemical company at that time. This company also was a big producer of nylon resins for molding. At the time, I thought that nylon resins would have made a good combination with our Cycolac ABS in the United States. At that time, nylon was a molding product that was used only in Europe and its use really did not exist in the U.S. as a molding compound.

After setting up a project with BASF to form a joint venture in the United States—which would involve Marbon Chemical in this major European chemical company—Beré went to Europe to talk to their top management. This was after BASF and I had already worked out a deal. According to the European company's report to me, Beré seemed to make a real fool of us, although the Europeans were too modest to tell me what Beré said or did. As a result, this joint venture was never concluded. I have to blame Beré for that failure.

Beré ultimately decided he wanted to privatize Borg-Warner, and he did so with money mostly coming from Merrill Lynch. But after Merrill Lynch went after Borg-Warner to get their money back, Beré finally decided to sell Borg-Warner Chemicals. I tried to get one of the big Japanese chemical companies to buy us, but eventually they balked at the amount of money it would have cost them. It might have been worth it, though, because I think it would have given them a major foothold for operations in the United States.

Beré, as he told everyone, was a born again Christian; I'm suspicious of any kind of born again anything. It turned out to be right in the case of Beré; he seemed to me never to be really straightforward.

ANOTHER THING THAT BOTHERED ME relates to Bill Suiter, who had been president of the chemicals group. When Bill Suiter and I had lunch with the then-executive vice president of Borg-Warner, he told Suiter what a great job he was doing. Three months later, Beré had come to me to have lunch with him. As it turns out, Bere wanted me to tell him what I thought of Bill Suiter. I said to him that he had never talked to me about Bill Suiter before, so why ask all of a sudden now? I was a good friend of Bill Suiter and never would say anything negative about him.

Some background. Suiter had been trying to diversify with some small companies that fabricated plastics. Unfortunately, over a year or two these companies had not been profitable. So Borg-Warner decide to fire Bill Suiter. This was just three months after he had been told what a great job he was doing. This also soured me on the company.

Tom Farmer was Bill Suiter's successor as president of Marbon Chemical. Marbon's name was then changed to Borg-Warner Chemical because the Chicago office wanted all companies owned by Borg-Warner to carry the Borg-Warner name. These Borg-Warner divisions advertised themselves as the five hats of Borg-Warner.

I WAS REALLY TURNED OFF BY BERÉ and decided to retire from the company in 1982.

Prior to my leaving, Mr. Beré sent our top legal officer, Mr. Russell Parsons, to my office to talk to me. This gentleman seemed to be beating around the bush. I wasn't quite sure why Beré had sent him, but I expect the reason was he thought that I might sue Borg-Warner for discrimination. Tom Farmer had indicated to me that I didn't get the president's job of the chemicals group because of my religious affiliation, despite having been Vice President of Borg-Warner International. As I recall, I told Mr. Parsons that I knew and respected him as a great, great individual and how negatively I thought of Bere. I also told him that he knew me better than for me to try to pull something on the company. I practically told him to tell Beré to go to hell.

PART 3
LIFE BEYOND PLASTICS

Chapter 16
Try, Try Again

After I retired at age 62, I decided that I wanted to do consulting work and share with other companies what I learned about business.

Through the financial officer at Borg-Warner, I was given good contacts to all the major investment banking firms in the U.S. The reason I was interested in the investment banking industry was because I had watched over the years how the investment banking firms operated. I saw many instances of the poor help they had given companies that wanted to form joint ventures. I knew from experience that most of those joint ventures were going to fail.

Nothing I tried for getting consulting work worked out. Most of the investment banking firms did not even consider my working with them. The closest I came to going to work for any of these firms was with Merrill Lynch, but that also finally fell through.

I went to Boston to Arthur D. Little to say good bye to the people I knew there. Even before my visit there was over, they offered me the job of setting up an Arthur D. Little office in Chicago. I considered their offer as an interesting possibility, given the good reputation that Arthur D. Little had in the U.S. at that time. This job eventually fell through, though, because the two departments that were supposed to pay for the Chicago office couldn't come to the decision to pay that extra money to support it. So there I was, back at step one.

I went to talk to most of the better-known consulting companies in the country, of which I thought Boston Consulting was the best. It had been started by an employee of Westinghouse Company.

What I finally figured out from all this effort was that in most instances, each of the consulting firms I came in contact with had to look for new contracts every three months or so. The consultants for whom they had no work were just sitting on their behinds. Of course, their clients ultimately paid for all that idleness. This process was, to me, wrong for two reasons: first of all, I didn't want to have to look for new projects every 3 months; secondly, I didn't think that it was right that the potential client wound up paying for those employees of the consulting firm who were idle because they had no project to work on.

So my decision was to go out and, without charging the potential client too much, propose to work on a long term arrangement. The agreements included the possibility that when more than just myself was needed for the work that they required, we would negotiate separately on an agreed-on contract for the additional person(s).

After A.D. Little and the investment bankers had fallen through as possible employment for me, I wrote about 85 or so letters to the heads of all the chemical companies that I knew around the world. I told them that I was retiring and going into the consulting business.

I had always been considered by the people at Borg-Warner Chemicals as someone who knew everybody important in the world in chemical businesses. As I mentioned before, this was because I made a point of meeting with the top officers of these companies each time I visited overseas or even when I was travelling in this country. You never knew when the time might come that we might do something good for either one of our companies.

As a result of this practice, everybody in the chemical industry knew that I knew everybody in their industry. I could never understand why everybody else didn't do the same as I did.

I got answers to probably 80% of those 85 letters I wrote. Everybody wished me good luck and told me how well they thought

I would be doing, but nobody came up with an offer to go to work for them.

Chapter 17
International Consulting

The first consulting offer I finally got after retirement was from Ube Cycon. My job was to write monthly reports for them on what was going on in the world.

It took me about 2 years to find another 5 or 6 companies to work with. These were primarily in Japan but there were also a couple in Europe and in the U.S. I negotiated contracts with these companies, charging about $500 a month, with the understanding that the contract would continue for at least 3 years. As I said earlier, there was also a provision for revising the contract so that if any project needed more than just me to work on it, we would negotiate a reasonable amount of contribution for additional associates of our consulting company.

One of my Japanese clients asked me to visit one of their plants in China, so I made my second trip to China in the late 90s. It was quite a contrast from my first trip in 1974. You can read an account of that trip in the Appendix.

CHINA. The plant that I visited was closer to Shanghai than other cities, so my trip resulted in my staying in Shanghai and traveling maybe a hundred miles or so to the client's plant.

I was overwhelmed at what I saw in China. The architecture of the new buildings that had gone up (and were continuing to be built since my last visit) were absolutely fantastic in appearance. These buildings were more impressive than any I had seen anywhere else, including in Berlin, Germany. After all, Berlin was also rebuilding after the war, but in comparison to Shanghai, the Berlin buildings looked very ordinary. When I asked the Germans why they didn't have new ideas on how to build great buildings, they told me that the decisions of what buildings could go up in Berlin were all made by committee. This view indicates again what committees can do in a positive way and where they completely fail.

In addition to the architecture, I was impressed by my stay at the Hilton Hotel in Shanghai. It was the best run Hilton Hotel that I have ever stayed in, anywhere. I was so impressed with the service and the food that I talked with the manager about how he was able to offer such services. He told me that the number one reason was that the Chinese were not very good at giving service so he hired all his people from Hong Kong. He really had a terrific capability of building an environment in which they could give such great service. I talked also to the cooks and the chief of the food department and was really impressed with how dedicated he was in offering the best to all their customers.

Of course the environment in China had changed a great deal since my first trip in 1974. No longer were the blue jackets in sight and so the people looked much more colorful. It was easier to have conversations with them because surprisingly quite a few Chinese people now spoke English.

We visited a town about 2 hours drive from Shanghai. There were a lot of big gardens with all different kinds of flowers and trees and bushes. It was a town which had become a major manufacturing enterprise.

We visited various gardens in which there were little houses. We discovered that these houses were used on weekends by some of the richer men of Shanghai. They sat around drinking tea, watching the women go by each night (with whom they hoped to have affairs).

TAIWAN. The Australian company, the one that we at Borg-Warner had a joint venture with, had another joint venture for making ABS resins in Taiwan. It was called the Taita Chemical Company. The Australian company asked me and Jim Spainhour to go to Taiwan to help them with upgrading their process. So for several years we went at least once a year to Taiwan, primarily to Taipei and to a southern city where the plant was located.

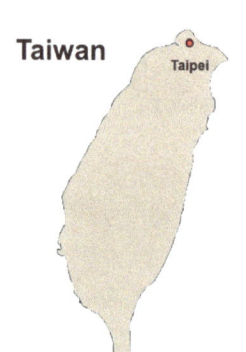

Taipei to me was nothing special except for an art museum that had ancient ceramics on display. Many of them were quite fascinating; some of the ceramics were 5,000 years old, which certainly impressed me.

The one thing I will never forget during a car trip in Taiwan was seeing a man on a motorcycle. Behind him was his kid and his wife; in the front, hanging onto the motorcycle and sticking his head way out in front was a dog. It was a fairly big dog. What a sight! I will never forget it. Unfortunately I wasn't able to photograph it.

Taiwan has some beautiful hills on which many people live, but other than that, Taiwan was not very impressive. Perhaps an exception is the view of the northern part of the Philippines, which you could see on clear days from the southern tip of Taiwan Island. However, I should note that some people claim that you cannot see the Philippines from the southern tip of Taiwan, and I've never been able to find out if you can or cannot see the Philippines from there.

THAILAND. Bangkok is a very, very captivating city. It's worthwhile to take time to see the temples and to ride on the boats on the river where there's a lot of commercial selling going on. The people of Bangkok are very friendly.

I met a lady who was a travel agent. She had a daughter who worked with her and a son who was in the Thai navy. Over the years I got very friendly with the family, being invited to their home for dinner. The daughter took me to all the significant places to see in Bangkok.

Thai food has a unique appeal. Also, there are many antique shops where I saw some very unusual pieces. I remember buying two silver birds which a shop had on display in the window. They didn't want to sell, but I finally convinced them they should sell the pair of birds to me. I still enjoy looking at them.

The mother spoke very good English. She went to Europe frequently to sell some of the beautiful Thai silks, primarily used for ladies' dresses. I brought home some Thai silk to have a dress made for Libby.

HONG KONG. In the 1950s and 60s it was very nice to stop in Hong Kong. Hotels, food, and goods were quite reasonable and a lot of people have suits and jackets made in Hong Kong.

I went to a tailor who was recommended to me by an Englishman who lived in Hong Kong. I had a cashmere jacket and a lightweight suit made there, but neither the jacket nor the suit really fit all that well. I would suggest to anyone who wants to have clothes made in Hong Kong to be very careful in selecting a tailor. While clothes are a little cheaper in Hong Kong than they are in America, they don't fit the way American clothes are made.

I HAD TWO MISHAPS in Hong Kong. One turned out fine, the other I very much regret. The first was on a trip from Australia to Japan, with my usual overnight stop in Hong Kong. This was in the early days of the 747. It was customary for the airlines to put suitcases in big containers that were loaded in the belly of the plane. Unfortunately, this one time my suitcase didn't arrive with me on a British Airways plane. I later found out that it was in one of those big containers; that particular container went all the way to London. It took me about a week to finally have it returned to me in Tokyo.

Because of the hot weather both in Australia and in Hong Kong, I just traveled in a short sleeved shirt and some slacks. The next day, when I was going to Tokyo, I had a business meeting with about 20 or 25 people. Of course, I just couldn't appear at the meeting in slacks and a sport shirt.

Well, you have to make yourself known to the airline if you want something. You have to get on top of a desk and jump around for awhile until they notice you. When they did notice me, I told them about my predicament, that I had a business meeting in Tokyo–and no suit.

In those days, certainly if you flew first class, they paid attention to you. British Airways promised me that they'd have someone meet me when we landed in Tokyo and they would buy me a suit and shirt and tie. I don't think any airline today would consider doing this. Sure enough, when I got off the plane in Tokyo, there was a representative of British Airways. He took me downtown to one of the department stores, I think it was Mitsukoshi, to get me a new suit.

I started putting on some of these Japanese suits and the pants reached almost to my knee and the arms almost to the elbow. Then I see a sign "Balmain" on the other side of the floor. I said to the British Airways representative, well, obviously these Japanese suits don't fit me and we may have to go buy a European-made suit. He said, "I understand," and we went over to the European side of the floor. I tried on a Balmain suit, a nice gray suit, and it fit perfectly. So I said, "well, what are we going to do?" And he said, "well, we'll have to buy the Balmain." I thought the suit would be very expensive. As it turned out, however, it was made under license in Japan and it only cost $150. I enjoyed that suit for many, many years.

Another story of a suit in Hong Kong. The Peninsula Hotel in Hong Kong was a beautiful hotel, with beautiful big rooms, a nicely done restaurant in the lobby, and a Swiss bistro serving good European food.

It was really humid on one of my trips from Australia to Hong Kong. Because of the high humidity, my suit had sort of wilted. I asked them in the early afternoon to press the suit so it would look okay the next day, and the hotel agreed without any problem. They brought my suit back in the late afternoon and I hung it in the closet without a second thought.

When I got up the next morning and put on the pants, I saw that they had been burned. I called the management office and they said they would send somebody up to look at my pants. A man came and said he'd be back in a little while. That little while turned into a couple of hours. When he finally showed up to my room, he brought the old lady who had pressed my suit. He said that if I made any claims they would take it out of the measly salary that they paid this lady.

I was so upset that they would make such a threat that I immediately went down and talked to the Swiss manager of the hotel. I told him that, number one, I was never going to stay at the Peninsula again, and number two, for them to threaten me in order to punish a poor lady was absolutely outrageous.

I never stayed again at the Peninsula. It took me, I think, over six months to get a measly $150 from them for the damage. Of course, I never could wear that suit again. I remember telling all my friends never to stay at the Peninsula for what they had done to me.

That was one of my poorer experiences in Hong Kong. It was always good to visit Hong Kong, though, since I had a friend from business school who was the Far East manager for Parker Pens. He had a boat, so we went out at lunchtime, bought some shrimps and had lunch on the boat. We had a really great time.

I went to some of the restaurants in Hong Kong with some of the local people whom I got acquainted with. I never knew what I ate– and that was probably just as well. Nevertheless, it was always a fascinating experience.

It is also worth noting that when you went to some of the better restaurants with natives of Hong Kong, you always paid a lot less than if you as a foreigner went just by yourself.

Hong Kong since has gotten very expensive and is no longer the attraction that it was, but what I also enjoyed was a trip to the Chinese border where we saw across the border into China proper.

JAPAN. It was after I had retired when I learned that Borg-Warner sold the Kureha Chemical venture, which I mentioned earlier, to Rohm and Haas. I would never have done that. Why not? Because Rohm and Haas would have acquired the company at a very reasonable price and so they were able to just take a lot of cash to the bank.

Our Japanese counterparts in Ube usually had a very expensive supper. They played like children: dancing and singing and feeling very relaxed. At dinner time women on both sides of each guest would fill their glasses and to help them with their food and whatever other assistance they needed. This dinner ritual also happened in Tokyo, but the people in Tokyo were quite different from the people in the countryside, such as those in Ube.

When we were in Tokyo and went out to dinner, we usually went to a nightclub after dinner and were surrounded by hostesses. With the nightclubs closing at midnight, at about a quarter to twelve our hosts disappeared and you were left with the women. Western businessmen in Japan usually had a very bad reputation because the only women they knew were the hostesses in the nightclubs. When these western businessmen were invited to a party or a dinner, they brought these hostesses with them—stupidly, in my mind—to such affairs. As a result, these western businessmen developed a reputation which was hardly favorable. Unfortunately, many westerners made this mistake.

Wives were treated quite differently in Japan than I was accustomed to. In one case, the wife of the president of a Japanese company (I have now forgotten which one) sat in the car for 2 hours outside, without my knowing it, while we were conferring in the hotel; had I known, I would have brought her in. This was not a low-level employee, but a high officer in a Japanese company.

When we went to Japan we usually brought our wives; on the other hand, when we had dinner at night with our counterparts, they never brought their wives. We finally did arrange for the executives to bring their wives as well. The wives enjoyed those dinners very much and it became customary thereafter that the Japanese wives join our dinners.

When it comes to hotels in Japan, I stayed in the original Imperial Hotel, which was designed by Frank Lloyd Wright. Later I also split my stays in Tokyo between the new Imperial Hotel and the Hotel Okura, which was near the American embassy and the Ube Kosan office. The Okura in Tokyo is one of the best hotels that I've stayed in. Once they get to know you, you check in and you're in your room within 5 minutes after you get to the hotel.

Also, when leaving by bus to the airport, the general manager would always come up to me and say goodbye. This courtesy has not happened anywhere else.

I've never had anything but good food throughout Japan. I especially remember the best tempura I had. It was in a small diner in Ube City in the southern end of Honshu, near the southern island of Kyushu.

Hokkaido, the northern island was fascinating. It is less crowded than what you experience in Tokyo. I especially enjoyed the beautiful weather in the autumn when the leaves change color. The University of Sapporo happened to be built by people from New England. As a result, Sapporo in the university area looks pretty much like an American city.

Also, incidentally, Sapporo beer that is made in Sapporo has much better flavor than Sapporo beer that's made in Tokyo. Coincidentally, the latitude of Sapporo is the same as that of Munich, Germany and Milwaukee, Wisconsin, both cities well known for their beer.

ON A SOCIAL NOTE, PRIME MINISTER SHINZO ABE of Japan made quite a pronouncement in late September, 2013: one of his goals is to ameliorate substantially both the economical and societal position of Japanese women. It will be interesting to watch how this takes effect.

MICKY NAKAYASU. While I was at Borg-Warner, we met much of Ube Industries' Nakayasu family. The president's youngest son, Aiji, was sent to New York to run a New York office of Ube Industries for several years. We saw Aiji frequently in New York; we had met him and his wife Micky previously in Tokyo and became very friendly with them. Aiji seemed to be a pretty nice fellow, but Libby and I were most impressed with Micky.

In her younger years, Micky had gone to design schools in New York. In fact, she spent about nine years in New York before going back to Japan and starting her career as an interior designer and decorator. Over that period, she furnished the interiors of five or more hotels, the first one being in Kobe. She also furnished the interior of corporate enterprises, and the interior of a main building at a private golf course.

For every facility that Micky designed, she personally went to Europe to find and purchase the different pieces of furniture, stools, sofas, lamps, etc. for her clients. She was one of the most gifted interior designers that I was ever acquainted with. In 1998, she came out with an exquisite book in which she explains her work and shows pictures of her various designs. The book title is *"The Design Work of Micky Nakayasu."* It is a beautiful reflection on her taste, her capabilities and her reputation as an interior designer.

Micky built a very lush office in a building next to the New Otani Hotel in a famous part of Tokyo. Unfortunately, she spent a lot more money on it than she should have, especially as her assignments for interior design decreased.

To me, Micky Nakayasu became one of the more unique, successful designers and individuals that I have ever met. She bridged the differences and similarities between East and West better than any other person we have ever met. Quite a few years ago now, sorry to say, we lost touch with Micky, which is a shame.

Chapter 18
A Taste for Art and Cheese

During my travels around the world, I wanted to keep some memories of the different parts of the world I visited. The best way to accumulate those memories, I thought, was to buy some paintings, or prints, or even sculptures, mostly small ones.

I never paid much for many of them. I did, however, acquire one of the more famous ones, an abstract print by Marc Chagall. I also acquired a print of a famous Italian artist whose name I can't remember, and I also acquired prints by Victor Delfín and Miro that I was particularly impressed with.

There are other artists I appreciated, among them Andy Warhol. Before he got into abstract paintings, Warhol did some non-abstract work, which I thought was absolutely fabulous.

I think that we have assembled quite a wide-ranging collection of art with the hundred or so paintings, prints and a wall hanging that I have acquired, although the most valuable pieces are now in storage.

We acquired our first painting on a cross-country trip to California. It's the picture on the left at the beginning of this chapter. We stopped in the mountains in Taos, New Mexico. Taos is a famous artist village. Late one evening, we met one of the Taos artists in a bar. He asked us to come to his apartment, a small studio, to look at some of his work. We went to his studio, and after looking at some of his pictures, we picked one about 3 feet by 6 feet. It was abstract, more-or-less, and you could read some of the history of his life in this painting. We thought this painting was very interesting and we only paid, I think, $40 for it, just enough for him to live on a few more weeks. We trekked this picture in our car, all 3'x 6'of it, all the way to California and back to the Midwest.

A lot of my friends who looked at this painting had various comments on it, but Libby quite well identified the various scenes on the picture that represented this artist's life. On the other hand, a very well known English gentleman friend of ours who came to see it said, "Oh, it looks like Custer's last stand," and had a good laugh about it. So this was the very early beginning of a varied collection of paintings, prints and small sculptures that we acquired throughout our decades of travel around the world.

The question obviously arises: Why was I attracted to art?

As I tried to think about that, I remember that my mother's closest girlfriend in Munich was married to a painter. He primarily painted landscapes. I recall that my mother acquired several of his paintings. They were probably pretty good but weren't of particular interest to me.

The art that got me most interested in over the long term was abstract art. I felt (and still feel) that if you look at a piece of abstract art, you get a new impression of it every time you look at it. That aspect of abstract art fascinated me.

At one time I was considering doing some of my own painting and bought some oil and water paints and an easel. One day, in the 1960s or so, I started outlining an abstract center or city-type of painting. It was in water color, using different color schemes. It's the picture on the right at the beginning of this chapter; I probably modeled it from the picture at the top of chapter 13.

I finished it in probably 4 or 5 hours. It was the first -- and last -- painting I ever did. People look at it and think it's quite, um, "interesting."

AMONG THE ENLIGHTENING EXPERIENCES one gets through travel is that one gets exposed to certain foods that aren't necessarily available in the United States. Cheese is one such food that has many regional varieties.

I got to liking cheeses in Europe. While quite a number of cheeses are being made in the northeastern part of the United States and in Wisconsin, the only cheese that I feel worth eating in the United States is cheddar, New England cheddar, especially the somewhat stronger cheddar.

There is no comparison to the variety of cheeses that are available in Europe. I need to emphasize that the cheeses that I will mention by name in this chapter are the ones that I prefer. These come from several countries in Europe. Of course, there are hundreds of cheeses made throughout Europe, and other people may very well have other preferences.

There are four countries in particular that make some cheeses that I like very much: Holland, Italy, France and Switzerland. Following these are Germany (particularly southern Germany, which makes some very tasty cheeses as well) and the U.K.

There are, of course, good cheeses also made in Scandinavia, although I don't name them specifically. There is plenty of cheese in Greece, but I have no taste for Greek cheeses.

In Holland, there are three cheeses that I find tasty, among the many available: Gouda, Edam and Leerdammer. The last one is quite a bit like Swiss cheese.

As you probably already know, until just in the 1980s and 1990s, Japan for instance had no cheese available, and I know really nothing about cheese in either South America or Africa.

So, these are some of my personal thoughts on cheese. Others may differ, but I believe that we have outlined a very good, broad review of the cheeses that are readily available in Europe, but surprisingly, not in the United States.

Chapter 19
Personal Observations on Europe

DENMARK. I did not spend too much time in Scandinavia, but there are a few things probably worth talking about. A major reason to go to Copenhagen was that Lego, one of Borg-Warner Chemicals' first major customers, was not too far from Copenhagen. The first number of times I went there, they didn't have an airport and we had to spend several hours going overland by car. This offered a great opportunity to enjoy the views.

Copenhagen's hotels had quite an unusual arrangement for a room with twin beds. The rooms themselves were narrow and long and the beds were placed head to head, rather than next to each other. This is a unique arrangement that I had never seen in any hotel anywhere else in the world.

Copenhagen's restaurants had very good diverse food. Their herring is unmatched. There were many bars in Copenhagen, but the one that I sticks in my mind was a gay bar; it had an older lady who sang French songs so fantastically that I would compare her to any of the best French chanteusses in France. This bar was a place we always went to when we were in Copenhagen. For entertainment outside of bars, Copenhagen had very nice museums and Tivoli Gardens, which was worth going to a few times to see the diverse entertainment offered. There also was a wonderful museum north of Copenhagen that had fantastic sculptures in a garden that I had hardly seen anywhere else except in Oslo, Norway's capital.

NORWAY. We were taken by representatives of Borg-Warner Chemicals in Norway to one of the beautiful fjords near Oslo where we had lunch. The salmon I had was white and had a wonderful flavor. In general the salmon we get in the United States has an aftertaste that I don't like, and therefore I never eat salmon here. But the salmon we had that were caught fresh in the Norway fjords was absolutely fantastic.

SWEDEN. I met a fellow on the plane from Australia to Hong Kong when I was stationed in Amsterdam. He invited me to his home in Gothenburg, Sweden, over a weekend.

We went from Gothenburg to the southern shore of Sweden to visit a small house that was owned by this fellow's father. He dared us to go into the water. I like to swim, but the water there was so cold that I could only stay in for a few seconds before escaping.

That weekend visit turned out to be a real "lost weekend." The fellow picked me up at the airport. First we went to lunch, had beer and one of the Scandinavian aquavit-type drinks. In the afternoon we went to his house and had more drinks. In the evening he took us out to dinner with some of his friends, where we drank more wine. Then, after the dinner and the wine, we went to his house and he presented us with a midnight dinner and some more drinks. I didn't drink very much because I'm not used to drinking; I couldn't understand how the Swedes drink so much liquor and survive.

GERMANY. In Germany, I have a real liking for the southern part, compared to the north, from the Black Forest all the way down to Switzerland, and of course, Munich, where I was born.

Now, however, when I go to Munich, it's just a pleasant place to visit. I go to the city just as I would to any other city or country, forgetting about all the Nazi horrors that I should remember…but escaped from.

In Munich, I like to stay at the Mandarin Oriental Hotel, which was originally an antique place. It was converted as a privately-owned hotel and is now owned by Mandarin Oriental. The service in this relatively small hotel is absolutely outstanding and the people who work there try to do their very best for the hotel guests. You could see all over the city from a swimming pool on the roof. It is a very pleasant place to sit when the weather is warm; you can have lunch brought right up to you along with a nice pool to swim in. The hotel offers free sunglasses and suntan oil in the pool area. Remarkably, the beverages in the room refrigerator are also free.

Other famous hotels in Munich, namely the Four Seasons and the Bayerischer Hof, are nothing special compared to the Mandarin Oriental. In fact, at the conference that I attended at the Four Seasons, they tried to overcharge me for the room. All the prices for the rooms at the Four Seasons need to be published in the room itself.

THERE ARE WONDERFUL TRIPS ONE CAN TAKE from Munich into the lakes, south toward the mountains. There are various places once can visit, including Tegernsee and the Ammesee Lake.

One castle stands out among all the castles built by the Bavarian kings. It's only half finished because they ran out of money. Half the hotel and half the castle is all in brick, but the other half has wonderful rooms, ballrooms, bathrooms. It has the biggest bathtub that I had ever seen anywhere and very much worth visiting, especially compared to the famous Neuschwanstein, which I don't think is all that remarkable.

Another quaint castle is Linderhof, which I think is worth visiting. There are many smaller villages throughout the Bavarian southern tip and close to the mountains that are worth going to.

In Munich proper, there are two restaurants I recommend to everyone. One is the Franziskaner. It is more or less a long bistro. Anyone who visits it should taste the weiss wurst, which is a veal sausage. You just heat and eat after removing the skin. I think the best weiss wurst you will find anywhere is in Munich. Also try the mixed potato and gherkin salad.

The other restaurant is Der Käfer. There is the main restaurant itself, and then there are very nicely furnished smaller rooms. If you have two couples or so you can get one of these rooms to enjoy an evening of unusual and good food, appetizers from a long exhibition of smaller dishes and various other well-cooked meals. These are the two restaurants I recommend in Munich proper.

The nice thing about Munich is not only that it has not grown into millions of inhabitants, but the Bavarian kings, besides building castles, did a wonderful job in copying the Italian buildings in many, many ways. Munich, therefore, historically remains today as one of the cities in Germany that gained from the buildings that the Bavarian kings put up, the castles that they built and the general environment. This environment is much different from the north of Germany, like Berlin. The people in the North don't like the Bavarians and vice versa. This north-south relationship is also true in other countries in Europe, which I think is quite remarkable.

I BELIEVE IT WAS IN THE LATE 1980s or early 1990s that I was contacted by Daimler Benz in Germany to come to Stuttgart to talk to them about plastics. They contacted me based on a recommendation that came from someone, in the United States. Unfortunately, I never found out who made the recommendation.

When I got to Stuttgart, I spent several hours with their top engineers. They were interested in the potential use of plastics for their cars. I was surprised how little they really knew about plastics and I also don't know what decisions they came to after our meeting.

In the afternoon after our having gotten together to talk about plastics, they took me to the Daimler Benz museum in Stuttgart. It was fascinating to me. Daimler Benz had started with manufacturing motorcycles, just like BMW did, and then gradually moved forward to making motor cars.

In the 1930s Daimler Benz built several models of cars with art deco design. These cars were absolutely fabulous to look at—and I assume just as fabulous to drive. There were at least two models I saw that were so fantastic that I will never forget what they looked like. In recent years, the company did revive a model they called Maybach. It was a nice car, but it didn't compare with the ones in the museum. Apparently the Maybach was not attractive enough for Daimler Benz to keep it in their product line and they abruptly discontinued it. I think they stopped offering it nine or ten years ago.

The fascinating thing to me was that a bronze plaque remembering the holocaust was displayed in the main building at Daimler Benz. As far as I know, this is the only major German company that ever displayed such a memorial. This raised my opinion of Daimler Benz as being a very responsible manufacturer.

ERNST MOLTER. I met Ernst Molter when I first started consulting. The president of a German specialty chemicals company invited me to do some consulting for him in Frankfurt, Germany. As it turns out, the head of the German company was on the same board as I was of a small plating chemicals business in the United States.

At the time I met Ernst, he was one of the co-directors of the German company and we quickly became fast friends. I admired Ernst because, although he did not have a PhD, he had moved into the senior management circle. In Germany, this advancement is practically impossible for anyone without a PhD. Fortunately, the president of the German company was a very fair and smart individual. He recognized the value that Ernst contributed to the fortunes of the company.

Ernst to me was not only a very pleasant individual, but he was also smart and inventive. Recognizing his abilities, his company sent Ernst to solve critical business problems that needed to be taken care of. Actually, I believe Ernst took care of a great number of these critical circumstances. This is what made him so valuable to the company.

Ernst and I have known each other now for probably over 30 years. We talk frequently by phone, and we meet every time I'm in Europe. He since has retired to a modest house in Provence, France. While his main home is still in Frankfurt, Ernst spends a lot of time in Provence, taking advantage of what makes Provence so attractive to foreigners from everywhere: its countryside and relaxed living.

I have had many invitations from Ernst to visit him in Provence, but I have as yet not had the chance to make it down there. I hope I will soon.

Ernst and his dear wife made it possible for his son to go to the best schools and obtain an education that made him as of now very successful in the real estate business. This is another thing which I admire so much about Ernst: how he takes care of and makes very effective plans for his family.

SWITZERLAND. In southern Europe, Italy and Switzerland are my favorites. Since my business travels while at Borg-Warner were primarily during the first two months of the year, my family and I took a skiing vacation in St. Moritz, Switzerland every year for 8 or 9 years.

St. Moritz is thought of as extremely expensive. But just before the season starts in the second week of February, the prices overall are reduced by a third. These price reductions make it cheaper to go to St. Moritz if you're there in the wintertime than it is to go to Colorado in the United States. For me, St. Moritz is absolutely the best place to go to in the Swiss Alps. It is on the south side of the mountains and therefore gets much more sunshine than some of the other places.

We always stayed at the Kulm Hotel in Switzerland, facing the mountains. Its inside swimming pool was just so appealing and they had very good food. Every year the same people came at the same time as we did, so we made some good friends while there. I always preferred the Kulm Hotel to Badrutts, the one that was located somewhat lower and fancied by all the famous people of the world, but I never quite understood why. The hotel was so famous but I thought it was dark and its location not among the best. Besides, they weren't very friendly to their customers.

Libby did not ski, but I skied the Langlauf cross-country course every year. Some trips lasted 3-5 hours, from early morning until lunch time at our destination. It was great exercise and I think the view of the mountains from St. Moritz is so much better than anywhere else in Switzerland. Some guests who used to come to St. Moritz sometimes went to other places. But they always returned to St. Moritz. I recommend it as the best place to go to in the wintertime and it's not a bad place to visit in the summer as well.

The other cities in Switzerland that I like are Interlaken, from which one can take beautiful excursions into the mountains nearby. There is no car traffic in some of these places, making them wonderful to spend a few hours.

Zurich is a town probably worth visiting for some, but I'm not exactly impressed with it. One exception is the Baur au Lach Hotel. Located next to the lake, one can get wonderful meals there and enjoy the lake nearby.

There are other places in Switzerland I enjoyed. One of the most impressive ones is the museum in St. Gallen which is several hundred years old and which is an unusual place to visit. The beautiful library is well worth the visit, for both the buildings as well as its books. And it's not very far from Zurich.

Lake Geneva is another place that is very nice. Geneva proper, however, has a large Arab community and is surprisingly a rather dirty town. Lausanne, not too far away, has a very fine hotel in the southern part on the lake named Ouchy, where one can spend some very relaxing days.

Switzerland is, by far, the one country in Europe that does make very, very tasty cheeses. My favorites are Emmentaler, Gruyere (aged Gruyere is better) and aged Appenzeller.

Fondue is a specially pleasant meal in Switzerland, and a lot of Swiss restaurants have their own secret recipes. While one particular type of Swiss cheese is used for making fondues, the best ones are those that are made with generational secret recipes.

Speaking of "secret recipes," I have had my own secret recipe for making cheese spread, which would last for several weeks when refrigerated. They were based on two packages of Philadelphia cream cheese, a pint of sour cream, a finely chopped yellow onion and little bit of dill powder and basil. It's not exactly a secret anymore, is it? My family and visitors always enjoyed this recipe, and I recommend you to try it as well.

ITALY. From St. Moritz it is possible to take a bus trip to Milan, which takes only a few hours. Milan is one of the famous starting points for visitors to Italy, with its big cathedral, but otherwise Milan is a rather commercial city. Some villages nearby are wonderful places and the lakes, like Lake Garda and Lake Como are among the prettiest places in Italy. Villa d'Este at Lake Como was quite memorable: in fact, we had a bathroom with a balcony!

One can drive along Lake Como all the way up to St. Moritz in Switzerland, with beautiful views all the way along the line.

The other part of Italy that I enjoyed most was Portofino, which is not very far from Genoa. An unusual experience we had was that coming from Milan, we had to change trains in Genoa to get closer to Portofino. The train was terribly crowded and I bitched because I couldn't get a seat. There was a gentleman near me who heard what I said.

"Don't worry, the next station is where most people get off and you'll get a seat."

The next day in Portofino, we stayed at the Hotel Splendido. The hotel has the absolutely best view of the blue waters of Portofino because it's on a hill. It was raining, and since we decided there wasn't much to do there, we went to Genoa to look around the city. Lo and behold, the same man we met on the train the night before was coming toward us. We both recognized each other. He said, well we have to have a drink. We did, and we became friends with him and his family for many years after that.

The man was Dutch, married to a southern Italian princess and had three wonderful children. He was selling a Scandinavian newspaper in Italy and so was pretty well off. One fortunate thing for us was that he was a member of a commission in that part of Italy that approved the ratings of the various restaurants in and around Genoa. Every time we went to Portofino, he took us to one of these small, but well-rated restaurants. As a result, we got to know that part of Italy very, very well. In fact, his children visited us when they came one year to the United States and stayed with us.

Unfortunately, we could not find him one year when we tried to contact him. He and his family had completely disappeared; our Borg-Warner office in Milan could never locate him, so that was the end of that particular friendship.

Rome is an extraordinary city and various parts of Rome are beautiful. Some of the hotels are well known, along with the Via Veneto, where people sit in outside cafes. In Rome, the one hotel that we enjoyed the most was the Hotel Majestic. It was not too far from other, more famous hotels. The Hotel Majestic, while old fashioned, had beautiful rooms. They were well- decorated, big rooms for entertainment; the hotel employed a man who gave counsel to guests at the hotel on where to go and what to see. This was very helpful to us. It takes quite a while to get acquainted with the various famous sight-seeing places in Rome, so it's always good to have a local there to give you advice. Otherwise, you would never finish what you should see in Rome.

As for Italian cheeses, I particularly like Fontina and Gorgonzola Dolce.

FRANCE. When traveling to France, Paris is the usual start. The first annoying experience is taking a taxi from the Charles DeGaul airport to whatever hotel you're staying at in Paris. It's a long distance to the middle of Paris, and one needs to watch the fare. Half-way into the city, the fare goes lower than what the fare is originally from the airport. Everyone should watch that the original A fare from when they arrive should change to a B fare.

Paris itself is one of the great places, obviously, to see in the world. One can spend a great deal of time just walking around Paris, sitting in the beautiful parks or seeing the grand museums that Paris has to offer.

There are many museums, many parks, many department stores, all of which are worth visiting. When going to the museums, it is always good not to stand in line waiting for tickets but to buy the tickets ahead of time. Saves you all that waiting.

It is also good to have some friends who can take you to the outlying areas around Paris such as Versailles because of the beautiful scenery and good restaurants to visit. There is a hotel right in the heart of Versailles. It was a very nice place to stay, but they tried to overcharge me from the posted price in the room.

We always stayed in small hotels. The Hotel Cambon, on the Rue Cambon, is one where we often stayed. Although the rooms are small, it's extremely well located, right in the center of Paris.

One trip which we will never forget was the one we took in the middle of France in the Dordogne area, east of Bordeaux. There are nice antique villages with hills all around, great restaurants and great small hotels. Their prices are half, or even less, than they are in Paris. A lot of English people bought retirement property in Dordogne. I think that many Americans would feel very comfortable there. Fortunately, I had a friend in Paris who went with us and did all the driving. It's someplace that everybody who visits France ought to go to at least once.

The other place in France that is well known is the French Riviera. It is very beautiful in many ways. The best place to stay when you visit there is in Nice. One can take bus rides from Nice to everywhere else. It is very hard to find a place to park; the buses aren't expensive, however, and they run everywhere from Nice out to Antibes and other places nearby. Personally, I prefer the Italian Riviera. Places like San Remo are much less expensive, and are just as beautiful as the French Riviera or Monaco.

France is famous for food, of course, but it helps to have local friends who know the mama and papa restaurants in town that are worth going to. The bigger restaurants that most foreigners go to are much more expensive and not necessarily any better.

To find out just what cheeses one has never tasted before that might be individually enjoyable, go to one of the restaurants in Paris that serves only cheese (fromage). One such place is Pain Vin Fromage. After you have lunch at such a cheese restaurant, you will have tasted between forty and fifty different type cheeses, ranging from soft and hard. These cheeses are accompanied by glasses of various wines that complement the cheese. I suggest that if you're ever in Paris and are curious about cheese, find a restaurant for lunch that specializes in cheeses.

In France, to get good Camembert, one has to go to northwestern France. It is only there I found a really good Camembert, in Normandy. To be enjoyable, Camembert must almost flow like a viscous liquid. I have never had Camembert like that anywhere but in Normandy.

The other French cheeses that I like are Port Salut and Chevre. Others, such as Gruyere, are not nearly as tasty to me as the Swiss versions.

UNITED KINGDOM. I used to go to England several times every year because of business relationships, but have not been there for a number of years now. London, in particular, has gotten so expensive that, in my experience, it's not really worthwhile if you're watching your budget.

But I enjoyed parts of England tremendously. Scotland is special because the people are extremely friendly. We located a Borg

Warner Chemicals plant in Scotland primarily because I could communicate with the Scots better than with the people in the south of England. At times, though, I find it extremely difficult to understand Scottish accents.

Edinburgg is one of my favorite cities in the U.K., not only because of its historical structures, but also because of its botanical garden that everyone should visit. Enjoy its beautiful trees.

Other parts of England that I've enjoyed: the Cotswolds, with its bright green hills, small, cozy hotels and restaurants. Don't miss Stratford on Avon. When you watch Shakespeare plays in Stratford, U.K., they are so different and exciting compared with anywhere else, including the Stratford in Canada.

Despite its high costs, London is certainly worth visiting for all its historic sites, military parades and the theater. I found two hotels in London that I particularly like. One is in Mayfair, called the Chesterfield, which has not only good service and a cozy bar, but it is the only hotel I found in London that picks up its guests at Heathrow Airport at a reasonable price.

The other hotel that I always enjoyed is the Conrad Hotel in Chelsea, close to the Thames River. You can see the river from the hotel and walk along the riverbank. The rooms are all suites with balconies; you can be very comfortable there, especially since you are not surrounded by concrete.

In terms of London restaurants, I enjoyed the Wolseley Piccadilly. It was named after the Wolseley Automotive Company, which went bankrupt in 1928. Two other restaurant owners took over and converted it to an excellent restaurant, keeping the same name, Wolseley. At that restaurant, I enjoyed the best codfish that I've ever had anywhere in the world and recommend it highly.

The other restaurant which is always enjoyable to visit is the Bibendum. It was built in a converted Michelin tire warehouse and we always enjoyed unusual food and exceptionally good service.

Another restaurant that I enjoyed is The Gay Hussar, an old Hungarian place where the socialists used to meet in the '30s. It has the best veal goulash and sour cherry cold soup of any of the Hungarian restaurants that I've been in anywhere else in the world. It's located near Haymarket Street in the Theater District.

If you want to go shopping in London, I can recommend Harrods Department Store and Selfridges. Of course, both of them are famous; once or twice a year they have sales in which goods are marked down by as much as 50%. One sale is in January, and I think another sale is in the summer. If you want to buy goods at a good price in the U.K., you should do it during those sales weeks.

As far as the famous clothing and textile makers in London, I feel that their goods are over-priced. It's not necessary to buy the mostly-heavy clothes that you get from British tailor shops.

Some of the tasty cheeses are famous in the United Kingdom. I should also mention that some cheese are better than others, even though they share the same name. The most famous of U.K. cheeses, of course, is cheddar, which originated in the Cheddar Gorge area in the county of Somerset. Cheshire, Red Leicester, Wensleydale, and Double Gloucester are other popular cheeses. Stilton is a famous cheese that is a bit like Gorgonzola. It's a whitish-yellowish cheese with blue veins running through it (there is a variety called White Stilton that doesn't have the blue veins, but the blue Stilton is the classic one). There are also Caerphilly, Derby, Lancashire and several others that you might want to try.

ORIENT EXPRESS. I believe it was early in 1987 that the Orient Express from London, England, to Istanbul, Turkey, was resumed after the interruption during the Second World War. The Orient Express had always held a great deal of mystery to me and I was anxious to travel on it.

In making inquiries about the trip, I learned that the people who were knowledgeable about rail travel recommended only the short trip between London and Paris since it was almost impossible for two people to sleep in one cabin overnight. The cabins of the train were that small. By going from London to Paris, one had a memorable short trip with dinner and drinks in the bar service car, and therefore could get the Orient Express experience at a much lower cost than what it would cost for the whole trip.

When Libby and I went, it was in the early days and the cost from London to Paris on the Express was perhaps only a hundred dollars more than one could make the trip by flying. So on May 12, 1988, we boarded the Orient Express in London on the way to Paris.

We spent the first part of the trip in the lounge car. We met some interesting people to converse with, there after which we went to the dining car. It was beautifully decorated and we were served a sumptuous dinner.

Unfortunately, our trip was troubled by a strike between the ships on the channel that brought the railroad cars across the channel from Britain to France. This was followed by another unhappy experience, namely a railroad strike on the French railways. As a result, we arrived in Paris about 3 hours late. A good friend of ours had been waiting all that time at the Gare de Nord to pick us up. So all I can say is that the experience of the trip on the Orient Express is very exciting, but I recommend only a short part rather than going all the way to Istanbul.

SPAIN. Spain is a very beautiful country to visit. I'm not all that excited about the capital, Madrid, but I feel very good about Barcelona. Architecturally, Barcelona has all the Gaudi buildings, including the cathedral, which is still not finished. It also has interesting museums, a nice coastline on the Mediterranean and people who are very, very friendly. In order to enjoy Barcelona, you must have local people to guide you around, as we were fortunate to have in our Borg-Warner representatives.

I went to the Picasso museum in Barcelona, Spain, where some of Picasso's earlier work was exhibited. They were mostly hand-drawn prints and not as interesting to me, compared to all his later work.

One part not to forget in Spain is the southern coast, where the first time we visited, we went all along the Costa del Sol. At that time we saw only one building in Marbella, which happened to be a restaurant. Now, the whole Costa del Sol is built up with condos all over the place and it is not as nice as it was when we went there in the 1960s. We rented a car at the Costa del Sol to take us up to the various cities in between the Costa del Sol and Seville. We found unusual places everywhere, like the buildings in Seville, the waterfalls and the kind of buildings we discovered in Cordoba, where original Muslim mosques had been transformed into Christian churches.

Our driver told us that he had been the driver of the movie actress, Ava Gardner, who had retired there. She had become quite a drunk and he told us how, sadly, he had to bring her to her room many times and had to put her to bed. What a sad ending to such a famous and pretty lady.

PORTUGAL. From Spain we once took a flight on a 14-passenger plane into Lisbon. I had been to Lisbon several times by myself. I enjoyed staying at a hotel in Cascais not too far north of Lisbon, right on the coast. It had a beautiful view of the ocean and had extremely good food, and rooms in the hotel itself. In Lisbon proper, we enjoyed staying at the Ritz Hotel, which not only had a great swimming pool, but a very comfortable room and excellent service. Lisbon is a city that is up many hills and down, and a very pleasant place to be when it comes to delicious food and fado, the very famous Portuguese songs one can listen to in restaurants and bars.

There is another city in Portugal, Coimbra, which used to be the capital and which is a couple of hours north of Lisbon. It is very much worth visiting Coimbra to spend some time, drink and see the castle located there. It has a beautiful view of the countryside.

MAJORCA. It is easy to fly to Majorca, which is the biggest island west of Spain. There are too many people in the South and middle of Majorca. The best place to stay in Majorca is at the northern end of the island, the Formentor Hotel, which is known for a book prize given there once a year.

My ex-neighbor in Parkersburg, West Virginia and I spent time in Spain and in Majorca. One year we stayed at the Formentor

Hotel between Christmas and New Year's. The hotel has about 200 or 300 rooms, but my friend and I were the only guests. Nobody comes there around the end of the year because there are only about 4 hours of sunshine between 10 o'clock and 2 o'clock. You can imagine a hotel with a hundred servants catering to two Americans for at least two days! A third man from Minnesota, a manufacturer of burial vaults, eventually joined us as a guest.

We had a great time riding Italian Vespas through the mountain roads around the Formentor Hotel. The front of the hotel faces the countryside, and the other side faces the ocean. So, going to any of the islands off Spain I would stay at the Formentor Hotel.

BELGIUM. After visiting Brussels a few times, my wife mentioned to me that she didn't like the fact that I was away so much. She came to Brussels with me at one point and found a beautiful coach house near the Brussels University. It had been built by the owner of the apartment house in front for his son to live in, but the son decided he didn't want to live too close to home and so the coach house was up for rent.

The coach house was ideal for us. It had double doors out to the garden, which was very well manicured by some of the relatives of the owner of the apartment house. We could sit outside in the garden when the weather was appropriate. The downstairs had a kitchen and a big dining room; the upstairs had a big bedroom and bathroom. It was ideal for us. It was close to the Borg-Warner Chemicals offices on the Avenue Louise. We enjoyed the almost four years that we commuted between Brussels and Chicago every three months.

During the period when Libby and I commuted between Brussels and Chicago, I got exposed to the very good artists in Belgium, among them the famous abstract painter Magritte. To my way of thinking, Magritte produced some wonderful artwork.

We were told many times of tourists who were very much impressed with Brussels. Because we lived there, we were very impressed as well, not only by the fact that the traffic was quite moderate, but also that the facilities overall in town were very special.

The mama and papa restaurants which we were introduced to by our friends from Solvay Chemical were in most cases much better than what you find in Paris, and obviously a lot less expensive. We enjoyed the big parks all around Brussels, where it was wonderful to walk in or sit and relax. We enjoyed tremendously the art museums in Brussels, and thought highly of the local artist Magritte. We think Magritte was one of the most unusual and creative painters in Western Europe during this time.

It was fun each weekend, on a Saturday or Sunday, to go to the antiques market. It was in one of the big squares in the middle of Brussels. We were able to buy copper pots and tea cans very inexpensively there.

This is a story I'll never forget: Our name and address was listed in the Brussels telephone book. After about four years, the Belgian tax authorities caught up with us and wanted us to pay income tax. Fortunately for us, it was about time that we went back, so we gave up our apartment in Brussels and returned to Chicago.

We never heard from the Belgian tax authorities again.

Libby and Howard Irvin, longtime supporters of Givat Haviva, at the Chicago reception for Maestro Barenboim

Chapter 20
Morocco, Egypt, Israel

MOROCCO. There was a time, I believe it was in the late 1950s, when you could fly from Chicago to Europe by way of Morocco for $50 more than flying direct. For some reason, Morocco really attracted me, so we decided to fly to Algiers, the capital of Algeria, from Chicago and spend a week or so driving from there through Morocco. I rented a car and found the roads quite good and the road signs very understandable.

Algiers just seemed like any another big city, so we quickly took off to Rabat, where the king of Morocco had this palace and stayed there overnight. We found the streets of Rabat quite clean and the palace building rather interesting, but the place that everybody told us to go to was Fez. The next day we drove several hours to Fez, where we checked in at the city's number two hotel. The next day we started driving around Fez.

Fez appears to be about 2,000 years old and it doesn't seem to have changed very much over that time. There's one thing that everyone, however, should remember: if you want to go sightseeing in Fez by car, be sure to take a local guide recommended by the hotel. Without a guide, a hired guide, you would be surrounded by others who want to be your guide and they won't give up under any circumstances. We found it necessary, finally, to stop at a police station to get rid of the bastard who was trying to annoy us for an hour or so. We finally got wise and hired a guide at the hotel, who took us through all the places to see, which were absolutely fabulous.

Artists lined the streets of Fez, skillfully handicrafting all kinds of containers and plates from brass and copper. Even with the artists along the streets, the town itself really looked like it was a couple of thousand years old. Very different from the big cities in Morocco. We believe you will find it very much rewarding to go to Morocco and certainly Fez if you can, to see the countryside and the local artists and local residents.

We finally spent a week at the Mamounia Hotel in Marrakech. It is one of the older hotels in Morocco but the most famous one. Winston Churchill used to stay there almost every year. We ordered and got a wonderful room overlooking the swimming pool. We enjoyed very much the Moroccan meals, where you sat on the floor leaning against big cushions. Delicious stews are served in the restaurant.

There are parts of Morocco which, unfortunately, we were not able to visit. These were on the Atlantic coast, for swimming, and on the northern highlands, occupied by people who apparently had come originally from northeastern Europe. We very much recommend anyone who has the opportunity to visit all of Morocco, because it is indeed a fascinating country.

PAUL PINSKY. Through my friend Paul Pinsky from California and Hawaii, I was introduced to an Israeli organization named Givat Haviva. I have felt for many years that this organization is worth supporting, which I have done, because they are very active in improving Israeli-Arab relations.

Here is how I met Paul. Libby and I were on a holiday in Dubrovnik, Yugoslavia. A couple sat next to our table at breakfast time on the first day we were at the hotel. The couple lived in San

Francisco and were making the same type of visit to Dubrovnik as we were. As we started talking, I found out that the gentleman, Paul Pinsky, very much appreciated food and had been to perhaps 80% of the best restaurants in Europe that I also had been to. We quickly found out that we had pretty much the same taste, except, that in addition to food Paul was quite a wine connoisseur and probably was drinking the best California wines that you could buy.

As a result of that visit to Dubrovnik, Paul and I met frequently in Europe, frequently in London. We tried to see each other as much as possible. Paul turned out to be a remarkable personality, in fact, so much so that in 1997 Mr. George Engebretson, a native Hawaiian, wrote a book about Paul Pinsky and his contributions and accomplishments. I recommend "A Man of Vision: The Story of Paul Pinsky" to everyone to read, because it describes a very important innovator in many ways and at the same time a very straightforward, honest and self-deprecating individual.

Some background on Paul. He was born in Harbin, Manchuria, of Jewish parents and grew up in Manchuria. Paul met his future, lifelong wife on the train and got married soon after graduating high school.

Because there were many White Russian anti-Semites in Manchuria, Paul's wife arranged for him to get an American visa to go to school in Berkeley, California. Paul took a degree in animal husbandry and agriculture because ultimately he planned to move to Israel. The move to Israel never came about, however. Since what his wife wanted most was to get an American citizenship, Paul stayed on in California and went to work for a meat packing company for a brief time.

Paul was interested in relationships between people and the unsolved challenges that would allow people to move forward and upward and to obtain all the rights that individuals were supposed to have. He drifted into becoming research director for the AFL-CIO unions. After several years, Paul realized how incompetent corporations were in negotiating with unions, so he decided to turn around and become a consultant to companies regarding their labor relations.

To Paul's understanding, that incompetency resulted from the lack of responsibility that individual companies had, particularly in providing insurance to their workers. So Paul took on the responsibility of improving the conditions in various health insurance contracts. The need was truly great in Hawaii, where the pineapple and sugar cane industries controlled practically the whole country. Paul set up several insurance consulting companies and insurance businesses. And when it came to automobiles in Hawaii, his organizations probably became the biggest in Hawaii.

I admired Paul particularly because of his wide experience, his thoughtful thinking about innovation and his very modest behavior. Because of his background and experience with people on both the business and the labor sides, he gave stimulating parties in one of the best San Francisco clubs every Christmas holiday. He invited us to fly in from Chicago, and we always did. Those parties brought together diverse characters who were all his friends or close acquaintances. I don't think that mixture of people together happens anywhere very often.

As I mentioned before, Paul also was a great wine connoisseur. Whenever he took us to dinner in the San Francisco area, he went to small places where you brought your own wine. As a result, we got a great tasting of the best California wines that you can imagine. Because of his interest in wines, Paul even bought a wholesale wine company so he could make expense-paid trips to France every summer.

Paul was cheerful to the end but ultimately passed away quite a few years ago, very sadly for all humanity.

EGYPT AND ISRAEL. Givat Haviva has headquarters in the north of Israel. They run school classes for younger children, mostly between the ages of six and ten or twelve. Both Israeli and Arab children are in the same classes, to get them to trust each other and above all, to get better acquainted. Teaching these children are both Israeli and Arab teachers. The only thing they are limited by is the amount of money they can raise through volunteer contributions or from the State of Israel, because they also teach Arabic to the Israeli military.

Givat Haviva has an office in New York and for quite a few years they have offered reasonably-priced visits to Israel. Libby and I decided to go on one of these trips, probably in the early 1990s.

Our particular trip started with a few days in Cairo, Egypt, and about a week following that in Israel. I had heard that the taxi travel in Cairo was like taking your life in your own hands; fortunately I was able to reserve a car to pick us up at the Cairo airport, thanks to a lady in Chicago at a travel agency that specialized in the Middle East.

The trip became a little complicated because I was on business in Germany, so Libby had to take a separate flight from Chicago to, I believe, Rome and then on to Cairo. Both of our flights were supposed to arrive at about the same time. Fortunately, they did arrive around the same time and we were able to get the car that was waiting to take us to the Hotel Sheraton. From what I saw of the traffic, I was very happy that I made the arrangements that got us to the hotel safe and sound.

Among the other people that participated on the trip was, surprisingly to us, the young daughter of the assassinated President Anwar Sadat. She was very friendly. We learned that she lived in New England; she and Libby became quite good friends on the trip.

In Cairo, we made a few visits, one to the National Museum, where I saw some mummies. It cost some extra money to see these mummies, but I would say are not worthwhile, not impressive. The only other exhibit I saw that did impress me very, very much was a couple, dressed in white, seated on a bench. It was over two thousand years old, and yet the white looked as white as it possibly can and apparently it was that bright originally.

We went to the pyramids, which to me were unimpressive because they just looked like all the postcards you see. What did impress me very much was a very large, long boat made out of wood. It was held together completely by leather strips that were at least a thousand years old. That exhibit was more impressive to me than the pyramids or the sphinxes.

The Sheraton Hotel was really well run. One evening we saw an Egyptian wedding. Everybody was dressed just fabulously. It was fascinating to watch such an elaborate affair; we marveled at what it must have cost.

The only thing that I will never forget, food-wise, was that it was the season for guava when we were there in early October. The guava juice that hotel served was absolutely delicious, more so than any juice from any other fruit that I have ever tasted.

On the way to Israel, we got to the airport and found to our dismay that for some reason Libby and I were not on the manifest. We were concerned that we would have to sit overnight in that crowded, dirty airport in Cairo. Finally, somehow they got us on the plane and we arrived at Ben Gurion airport outside of Tel Aviv after only about a half or three-quarters of an hour flight.

From Ben Gurion Airport we were brought to a hotel south of Haifa. It was very comfortable and, much to our surprise, the service was perfect. I was surprised with that because, having been in Israel several years before, hotel service at that time was terrible...as was the food. It was a real contrast this time. The waiters were young and very friendly. Whenever we asked for something, the answer was always "no problem."

We went to some of the classes and met the teachers of Givat Haviva. This was very informative and gratifying to us. Because President Sadat's daughter was with us, we were received by many Arab households, who were all anxious to receive us, feed us and entertain us. She opened so many doors for us that wouldn't have possibly been accessible to us without her presence or her charm.

We went across the Israeli frontier into disputed west side territory and met one of the hotshot Arab military leaders. He was neither friendly nor impressive.

We were received in several Israeli government offices by some brilliant individuals whose names I've forgotten. I was surprised by the relatively low security measures that they took in these offices.

We traveled throughout the country, including the Negev desert area in the south where scientists were carrying on archeological digs. We went to Jerusalem, where we saw all the important areas of the region. We visited some of the Kibbutzim, where we had friends who had emigrated from the United States. It seemed that the Kibbutzim we visited were extremely well run and profitable.

So, under the guidance of Givat Haviva and the constitution of our delegation which included Sadat's daughter, this was one of the most memorable trips that we ever took in all our travels.

Kibbutzim have been very prominent in Israel since the very first times that the Jews, primarily from Eastern Europe, took over the country after the British withdrew and left the most strategic military positions in the hands of the Arabs. There was always a sort of anti-Semitism in England which did have quite an influence on the withdrawal of the British.

The number of kibbutzim and the people living in them has declined quite a bit as Israel's financial situation has improved. Part of this decline may be because many good scientists emigrated from Europe and joined research laboratories that foreign companies, including from the United States, have built up in Israel in the last two decades.

There are kibbutzim of all sizes; each one does different things, such as agriculture, manufactured items of all sorts and technical developments that they have exported to other countries.

While many profitable kibbutzim still exist, it is unlikely that new ones will be formed. It is possible that in future generations, many that are now in kibbutzim will have left them.

The initial Jewish immigrants had a really tough job taking over the country. They made all kinds of maneuvers to make the Arabs think that they had many more arms and people attacking them than there really were. They got the Arabs to withdraw and make it possible for the Jewish immigrants to take over.

In addition, the Arabs were advised by their military people that they should leave their homes in Israel because the Jews would soon be pushed into the sea. Once that happened, they could then take over the existing Jewish homes. Foolishly, a lot of Arabs took that advice and now are deprived of Israeli citizenship.

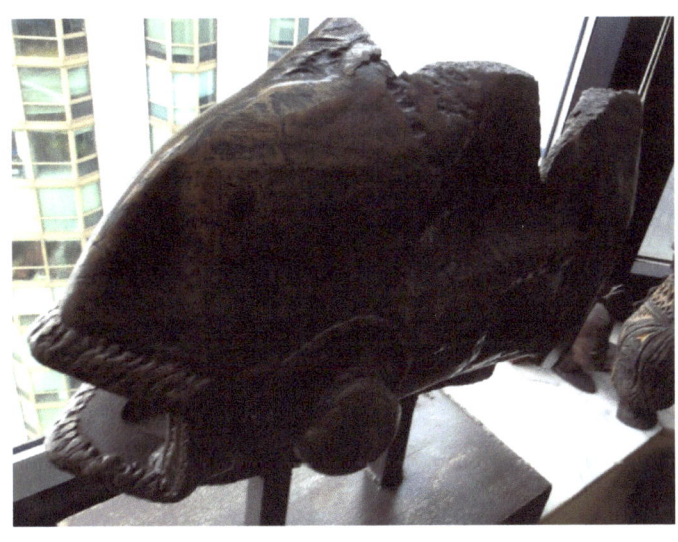

Chapter 21
South of the Border

JAMAICA. I believe it was in the 1960's that the Jamaicans were more friendly to Westerners than they were later, after they got a socialist administration. During those friendlier days, we took a 10-day or so vacation to Jamaica, based on a good recommendation.

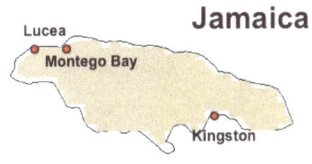

We arrived at Montego Bay by plane from the United States, and went by taxi about two hours west to the Sea Island Hotel in Lucea. It was a little less expensive than the more fabulous hotels on the north coast.

As it turned out, the Sea Island Hotel was the place to stay. In addition to the many United States and Canadian tourists, the local people who traveled the north coast used to like to stay at the Sea Island Hotel overnight. As a result, we met several local people who we very much appreciated getting to know, as they represented three entirely different classes of the Jamaican society. If you want to learn something about the country and its people, I think the Sea Island Hotel at Lucea is the best place to stay when going to Jamaica because that's where the local people stay. Here are examples of what I mean by three entirely different classes of Jamaican society.

The first man we met spoke perfect English, had gone to college at the University of Wisconsin and was operating a jewelry store in Kingston. He was very conservative and came across almost like an American. He was the least interesting of the three people I want to comment on.

The second man was relatively young. He had graduated from Jamaica University, had been the number one football player on the university team and had become a marketing executive for the best known locally-owned rum company.

He was very popular in the country, and whenever he appeared young children approached him, begging him for liquor. He was very upset because they were more interested in getting liquor from him than in getting an education. He also complained generally about the exploitation that American companies made in Jamaica. He took us to some of the local nightclubs to which he advised Westerners not to go by themselves. We were able to watch some very beautiful local dancing at those clubs. He was good looking, well educated, very smart and certainly represented his home country with great prestige.

The third and most interesting man, who stayed overnight a couple of times while we were at the hotel was Bobby Charlton. He was probably in his late 40s, as black as can be and he was, to say the least, very colorful. He was a terrific dancer. He could sit at our table for two hours telling dirty, funny jokes without ever repeating himself.

When Bobby learned that we were going home from Kingston, where he lived, he invited us to his home for dinner and said he would pick us up at our Kingston hotel. When we left Lucea, we took a local bus to Kingston. Our bus had not only colorful passengers, but colorful animals: chickens, dogs, and just about everything else you could think of.

When we arrived in Kingston, we called the number he had given us, and he promised to pick us up for dinner at his house. Bobby arrived at our hotel in a big Cadillac convertible, in which we learned he had driven Winston Churchill, the U.K.'s former Prime Minister, around Jamaica when he had visited the island a few years earlier.

Bobby was in the insurance business and a vice president of his company. He took us from the downtown hotel up to the hills in his convertible. Among the houses on the hills, women all along the street were waving at him. It turns out that they were in the prostitution business and all of them had their insurance with him.

When we got to Bobby's house, a servant opened the door. Bobby introduced us to his wife. She was white and had two teenage boys. Of course we were startled to see her and her two white sons living with a very dark black man. We learned that she became so fascinated with Bobby Charlton that she left her husband and moved in with him, with her children. They seemed to get along beautifully. About 9 o'clock, after the children went to bed, we had a sumptuous dinner. He then took us back to our hotel. We will never forget Bobby's personality. Later, we learned that Bobby became mayor of Spanish Town.

Of any of the other islands around the world that I had been to, I had never seen such lush nature, going all the way down, right to the rim of the water.

BRAZIL. I only visited South America once. Our trip started in Brazil. The purpose was to explore setting up a manufacturing facility in Rio de Janeiro.

When Libby and I arrived in Rio de Janeiro, our first disappointment was all the dirt and litter on Copacabana Beach. We were invited, however, to a beautiful apartment in one of the luxury buildings along Copacabana Beach. We enjoyed Brazilians and Argentinians at that particular party.

I could never understand a word of Portuguese during my visits to Portugal, but I was able to understand Brazilian Portuguese when someone spoke it slowly.

We also went to Sao Paulo; it was a jammed up city that seemed like a combination of Chicago, Tokyo and Mexico City.

ARGENTINA. From Brazil, we went to Buenos Aires in Argentina, which looks very European, but I was not very impressed and don't remember very much about that as a potential for a visit.

PERU. From Buenos Aires we went to Lima, Peru, in anticipation of going to Machu Picchu. We did very much enjoy Lima, not only for the hotel accommodations, but also for the food and quite a bit of the architecture and museums.

In fact, we were so much impressed with a local sculptor, Victor Delfín, that we bought one of his pieces. It is a fish created from an iron vessel hull and formed exclusively with a blow torch. It was similar to some larger sculptures he made that are not only in public places in Lima but in some South American museums as well.

Weighing about 300 pounds, the fish continues to amaze me that it could be made with only the use of a welding torch; it was fabricated completely out of cast-iron recovered from ship by a local (and now famous) Peruvian artist, Victor Delfín.

Delfín's large sculptures are on display throughout the city of Lima. We sought him out by visiting his studio outside of town and waited with his girlfriend for about three hours before he showed up. And even though we couldn't communicate very well with him language-wise, we did buy the fish, which was one of his smaller sculptures. Fitting 300 pounds of metal into our luggage was out of the question, so we had it shipped to us by air by Borg-Warner Chemicals representatives in Lima. We continue to enjoy that fish; it still sits in our window in our living room in Chicago.

THE LOCAL REPRESENTATIVES FROM BORG-WARNER not only invited us to their house for dinner, but also gave us advice about going to Machu Picchu. They gave us some pills to minimize the physical effect of flying from sea level to 12,000 feet in Cuzco.

We stayed in Cuzco overnight before taking a 3-hour train ride to get closer to Machu Picchu. Machu Picchu is actually a couple of thousand feet lower than the 12,000 feet that we encountered in Cuzco. Even so, the difference in height is so much that several of the people who were going with us to Machu Picchu had to stay behind because of terrible headaches. The pills that we had been given in Lima really helped us out. We arrived by train to a couple of thousand feet or so from Machu Picchu, and a car took us up the rest of the way.

Machu Picchu was only discovered, I think, in the 1920s by an American. It was an absolutely fabulous sight! Buildings had been put together by big stones fitted so closely together that you couldn't get a sheet of paper in between them.

At the time of our visit, I'm sure it was a much more rewarding experience than it is now. They have built hotels and other amenities which just don't live up to what the original buildings and construction of Machu Picchu present. If one wants to be close to heaven, this is absolutely the closest that I've ever come to being in heaven. Despite all the spoiling that has been done since we were there in the 1970s, I still recommend to everyone not to miss visiting Machu Picchu.

MEXICO. We often visited Mexico for relaxation early in the year because the western coast of Mexico was always sunny then and we would miss the rainy season. The weather was always good in late January or early February and fortunately it was not too humid.

Mexico City was a wonderful place to visit, not only because of the hotels and restaurants, but also for the culture, showcased by the exhibitions at the National Museum of Art. Many artists also live in Mexico City. A driver of one of the taxicabs that sat in front of our hotel promised us that he could introduce us to the artists. Although we were skeptical, we took his advice and he indeed brought us in contact with many of the local artists.

WHEN WE TALKED WITH ONE OF OUR FRIENDS in Mexico City, I told him that we had been in Brazil and Argentina. He said the one story people told in Mexico is, if you know an Argentinian for what he is worth, and you can sell him for what he thinks he's worth, you'd be an instant millionaire. That shows you what the people in Mexico think about Argentinians.

We went to a restaurant in Acapulco which is well known in the town. It was full, and since we had to wait for our table, we sat and waited in the bar. I started talking to a woman next to me. She said she comes down to Mexico all the time, and I said, Well that's fortunate for us; please tell us where we can go after dinner that the local people go to, not the tourists. She gave us two or three names. After we went through them, one of the places had more of a religious name, so we decided to go to that one.

Altogether there were three couples. I was on vacation and wanted to get away from business but one of the couples was a plastic machinery salesman from Cleveland who was there with his daughter. His wife had died a few months earlier. There also was a young couple from the East. We all piled into two cabs and they took us up into the hills.

When we got up the hills, girls came running up to us. It turned out that it was a whore house. It was the best whore house in the city, I learned. The girls quickly got three guys who were playing guitar.

"Why don't you send the women home and come back later?"

The daughter of the guy from Cleveland said, "Oh, it's interesting up here, so why don't we stay?" Libby said to her, "Well, your father can stay, but you come down with us. "

That was our experience in that particular Mexican town.

Chapter 22
Chicago People

It was quite a cultural change when we first moved to Chicago in 1960. Everybody asked me how I liked Chicago compared with West Virginia. I always told everyone who asked that question that Libby and I thought both Chicago and West Virginia were wonderful places to work and live, but the two are obviously very different and shouldn't be compared.

Libby and I rented an apartment in Lake Point Tower. At that time Lake Point Tower was the only high rise east of Lake Shore Drive, right on the edge of Lake Michigan. We got an apartment on the 53rd floor of this novel architectural development. We had a tremendous view of the Lake Michigan shoreline. Libby had always dreamed about living in a penthouse apartment in Chicago. The 53rd floor was quite a "step up" from her younger days when I first met her where she had lived in Indiana Harbor, Indiana. With our move to Lake Point Tower, we came as close to Libby's dream of penthouse living as we possibly could.

Well, a lot of people don't like Chicago because they think it's too cold in the wintertime and too windy the rest of the year. As for me, of all the big cities in the world that I've ever visited, I've always felt that Chicago, particularly downtown Chicago, is the most wonderful place to make a home. And the fall colors are beautiful, as you can see from the above photo of parks along the lakefront in the Edgewater area of the city.

In an interview in 2013, Mayor Rahm Emanuel expressed his thoughts on being mayor of Chicago. He said, "Chicago is not only a world city, but is the best city to live in." I fully agree with him. He expressed the idea that being mayor of Chicago is a lot better than being back in Washington, even as Chief of Staff to the president. It's better because in the environment of a city, you can do a great deal more than you can even in a high post at the White House.

We love living in Chicago. Downtown, without a car, you can either walk or take a brief taxi ride to almost everywhere you want to, to a variety of restaurants, shops and theaters (for which Chicago is well known and where new productions are tried out before they go to New York). Many major shows have had important starts in small theaters in Chicago before they went to the rest of the country, including Broadway. Chicago also has world-class museums, universities, hospitals, parks, and, of course, its magnificent lakefront.

There are fine hotels in Chicago, such as the Four Seasons. The hotel that I think is the best, however, is the Peninsula, These hotels are great places to stay in Chicago, AND at somewhat lower prices than in New York.

Chicago has great restaurants and you can find almost any ethnicity represented. The ones I particularly enjoy are the Shanghai Terrace Chinese restaurant at the Peninsula Hotel and the Chicago Brauhaus, which is one of the few German restaurants remaining in Chicago. The Brauhaus offers German food as good as as you would find in Munich in Bavaria. Spiaggia is a restaurant on North Michigan Avenue that serves the best risotto that I have ever eaten–amazingly, anywhere in the world. It's expensive, but should be tried by anyone who is in the mood for a fancy Chicago restaurant that also has outstanding food.

I could go on and on praising how nice it is to live in Chicago. Let me leave you with this thought: the friendliness of our people in Chicago makes it so much more relaxing and enjoyable than most other places in the world, and it is the people that more than make up for some of Chicago's more "interesting" weather.

I've lived or visited many times, over long enough periods, almost everywhere in the world except Eastern Europe. As far as the United States is concerned, I particularly like the people in the Midwest (and also in the South) because of their friendliness.

Some of the people I most admire have come from the Midwest. For example, Bob Shattuck who came from southern Indiana. A lady we called Aunt Louie, who lived into her 90s and was our baby sitter for many, many years came from Iowa. She had travelled with her husband, a famous entertainer, as far as Australia in the 1920s, and maintained her interest in world affairs up to her end. She was one of the most lovable people who I ever came in contact with. She represented the midwest genre to the best. She was known to all of us in the family as Aunt Louie, and to my family there could never be another Aunt Louie in this world.

TOM MINER. After I retired, Borg-Warner paid for a little office for me for about six months or so after I opened my consulting practice. My ex-boss at Borg-Warner, Jerry Dempsey, said that the Mid-America Committee had an office available in downtown Chicago and that I should talk to them about the possibility of renting an office from them.

The Mid-America Committee was founded by Tom Miner. It was supported by major businesses, law firms and individuals and perhaps even the City of Chicago for maintaining international relations that would be of value to Chicago in the long run.

Tom Miner came to our apartment one Saturday to look me over. He wanted to find out if I would fit into the space that he had in a very nice high rise overlooking the lake, right in downtown Chicago. During his visit that Saturday, we agreed on my taking an office at the Mid-America Committee.

I appreciated getting acquainted with Tom Miner, as he has had quite a history.

Tom was born in Southwestern Illinois, had gone to the Navy for a year, followed by going to the Army for another year, and then to

West Point for a year. Tom decided that he didn't like West Point because the first year he could not leave to visit family. And, after you graduate from West Point, you had to serve in the Armed Forces for at least four years. So Tom turned around and went to law school at the University of Illinois. He worked for about three different enterprises before he started the Mid-America Committee in 1966.

What amazes me most about Tom Miner is the number of prominent international personalities he has met during his presidency of the Mid- America Committee. He thinks that there were probably close to 200 of such distinguished people, among them Lady Thatcher of the United Kingdom; Mr. Gorbachev of Russia, with whom he was personally very friendly; Fidel Castro; all the presidents of China after Mao; he met three times with Henry Kissinger; and remarkably, with every president of the United States from Lyndon Johnson on.

In fact, Tom arranged three different trips to Washington for some prominent Illinois business people and politicians. I was fortunate to be on one of those trips. During that trip we met President Reagan, his general assistant Regan, and a few other people of the cabinet. I don't remember all the others that we met, but I do remember Paul Volker particularly. That's because he was smoking a very smelly, cheap cigar.

I'm sure that Tom Miner has met more politicians, by the way, including Ghandi, than most government officials in the world. He has been very modest about this, but to me it is almost incredible that he was able to establish these relationships. He is still very active and is now in his 80s.

To me he is one of the most remarkable individuals that I have encountered in my adult life.

JEFF DRIZIN. Jeff and I both had offices in the mid-America Committee suite, which is how we met. We talked often and became real friends in a very short time. Jeff came to the U.S. originally from the Baltic Republics and has been in quite a few businesses throughout his life, including textile manufacturing in Chicago. He is also involved in technical projects in Russia, where among other things he manufactures and trades in medical instruments. This has been a pretty good business for him. He travels to Russia a few times a year in order to take care of his investments there. He told me many times that he could arrange a very attractive trip for me to Russia, but I'm really not interested in going to Russia.

Jeff and I get together every month for lunch at the Brauhaus on Lincoln Avenue, one of the one of the best German restaurants in the city.

JOEL AND BARBARA HOCHBERG. Lake Point Tower had just opened when we first came to Chicago in 1968 and moved into the building. It was newly built and was just a few hundred feet from Lake Michigan, east of Lake Shore Drive. In fact it was the only building that was allowed to be built east of the Drive. We met a lot of delightful, friendly and well educated people who became residents of Lake Point Tower. The building's outdoor pool made it easy to make very good friends very quickly.

Barbara and Joel Hochberg were among the friends we made. Both Barbara and Joel originally came from the East Coast. Joel worked at the Leo Burnett advertising agency. He subsequently moved to Needham Harper Steers and later to DDB Needham. That company merged with another agency, Omnicom, which grew into one of the largest advertising agencies in the world.

At first, Joel worked as a copywriter at Omnicom and then became its corporate creative director. After a few years, Joel changed arenas and became president and director of marketing for Century Fox. This move turned out not to be his cup of tea, however, and he retired several years later. He and his wife settled in Rancho Mirage, California, where he had a beautiful apartment.

After his retirement, Joel started working—and has indeed completed— about 300 or 350 philanthropic charity projects. He does not get paid for these projects but graciously provides them to the charities. He lists the documentaries of which he is most proud: Finally!; Ishmael; and A Love Story in Cinema Verite Style. These are all available on YouTube.

Joel's wife Barbara has also been working for charitable organizations. She has formed a film group that meets and charges fees for the meeting. These events contribute around $2,500 a year to various charities.

Their beautiful daughter Lauren worked in Los Angeles, first in the film industry and then in a more charitable public relations firm where I believe she is now active. One thing unique about Lauren is that she was married twice. To the same man. The first time was in Hawaii, the second time at a relative's private island in the Caribbean. How romantic!

* * * * *

PERSONAL SERVICES. I want to briefly mention some individuals who helped us tremendously in our private lives.

The first person is **Dr. James H. Cohn**. Dr. Cohn practices at Northwestern Memorial Hospital in Chicago, certainly one of the best hospitals in patient care, not only in Chicago but in the country, with its excellent doctors and surgeons. To us, the most important physician there is Dr. Cohn, who received his degree from the University of Illinois. Dr. Cohn has looked after Libby and me since the early 1980s. He is not only a great diagnostician, but he also sees us every 3 months during the year and has a great personality in dealing with his patients. Remarkably, we have never had to wait more than 10 minutes or so for our appointments. We've been very lucky to have been introduced to him for our medical services.

I must mention my eye doctors who have served me for a long time. I've been going to **Dr. Robert Feder** and Northwestern Memorial Hospital in Chicago probably 30-some years. Dr. Feder removed my cataracts like an artist. It didn't hurt while he did it, nor did it hurt afterwards. At all. I believe Dr. Feder is considered the best cataract surgeon in Chicago.

Dr. Feder sent me to **Dr. Manjot Gill** in the ophthalmology department at Northwestern to deal with the macular degeneration that has set in. She has given me shots in the eye every eight weeks and has done a wonderful job in allowing me to keep reading.

Another person I want to mention is **Elliott Friedman**, who worked for one of the big international accounting firms when I worked for Borg-Warner. His firm was used by Borg-Warner Corporation for those Borg-Warner employees who spent a lengthy time overseas. Elliott eventually left his accounting firm to set up his own firm, Friedman and Huey Associates. When I retired, he agreed to take me on as a client. Elliott not only is very well versed in what the United States Treasury requires, but also the requirements of the Illinois State Tax authority. Elliott has given service to us since I retired in 1988, and we've had no problems whatsoever during that time. He is prompt, he is responsive and he is always accessible. That is remarkable for any kind of services nowadays.

Jim Michel, Sr. and his son **Jim Michel, Jr.** Jim Michel Sr. have been handling our investments since 1971. We have had the most excellent service ever since, no matter what larger firm he and his son were associated with. He currently is with Wells Fargo Advisory Services. Both Jim and his son have been dedicated to the most important needs of our family by assuring safe investments which do not fluctuate on a day-to-day basis.
In the great crash of 1987 our investments, fortunately, held very even because of the types of investments that Jim Michel made for us. He is not after trading very often in order to earn commissions, but he is really dedicated to serving us as clients. He is the most resourceful and remarkable stockbroker we have ever had. Over 40 years now, he has looked over our needs, and as a satisfied client we can only highly recommend him to you for safe investment services. I finally had the chance to meet Jim Michel Sr.'s wife

Marion. She impressed me immediately as a very fine, compassionate lady. I feel that she must have helped her husband a great deal in his career as a wonderful financial advisor and investment manager.

Mike Morelli is a prominent shoemaker in Chicago to whom I was introduced over 20 years ago. He operates the third-generation business Brooks Shoe Service, started by his grandfather. Mike is not just an excellent shoemaker; he is an artist because he can repair and reconstitute not only shoes but fabric-based merchandise, such as handbags and luggage. Over the years he has become a great personal friend and I admire him for his free spirit and so many innovative thoughts.

To me Mike is as self-educated as one could ever wish anyone to be. I enjoy his presence immensely. He has many important customers around the world, not only individuals but businesses like hotels and department stores and is unique. I would not feel that my mentioning good personal friends would be fulfilled without including him.

Another important person in our private lives has been **Rosalie Stanford**, who came to the United States from the Philippines. Rosie was introduced to us through another Philippine lady who worked for a neighbor. Rosie has been one of the most remarkable people whom we have been lucky enough to get to look after Libby and myself in all our personal needs. She not only is looking after us, making sure that we get the necessary medications that are prescribed by our physicians, but she orders everything that's necessary, she is an excellent cook and she does anything that's necessary for running our household. I really don't know how we

could maintain our private residence without Rosie and we're forever thankful that we were lucky enough to get her.

Rosie has a lovely 14-year-old daughter, whom she brought over not too long ago from the Philippines. Rosie's daughter is now going to school here and getting an excellent reputation as a student and has made friends in a very short time.

Chapter 23
Long-Term Relationships

I've been fortunate to have enjoyed long-term relationsips, some approaching 70 years. I've already told some of their stories. Here are some more of them, roughly in chronological order.

Paul Selow, who helped me by providing me an afidavit for me to come to America, was a wonderful, humorous, modest and most cultivated man that you'd ever hope to meet. I visited him for quite a few years, We became very fond of each other; he passed away in his early 80s.

Paul Selow had a relative in New York, a lady who was just as marvelous a person as he was. She was married and had a son who became the head of the International Rescue Committee, founded in 1933 on a suggestion by Alfred Einstein. It was a quite a famous social organization even back then, helping Jews emigrate to Israel; the organization also helped a lot of Blacks to immigrate from Africa, and they also helped southern Europeans. The son became a very good friend and I was very impressed with the services that he performed at the committee.

After the war, **Hans Lamm**, who helped get me an affidavit when I first came to America, returned to Munich and became the head of the Jewish community there. He also wrote a book about the Jewish community in Munich, which had approximately 6,000 people at the time I lived there. Munich had changed quite a bit after the war. Most of the Jews had traveled through Eastern Europe in order to return to Germany.

One member of the Rose-Hulman Board of Trustees, whose name was Berman, asked me to be on my alma mater's board. I believe it was in 1976. He worked as a representative of one of the major equipment companies in Indianapolis, Indiana. The Board, during all the time I was able to attend, had very good board meetings. Several of the Board members became very long-time friends of mine, particularly Jack Ragle. Several other long-term friends related to Rose Hulman: James Skinner, Harold Brown, Howard Freers, Mike Percopo, Abe Silverstein and Bob Shattuck.

I was given an honorary degree in engineering by Rose-Hulman in 1987 for spreading the technology about new plastic around the world. Getting this honor was a wonderful experience that I will never forget.

Women were finally allowed to study at Rose in 1995 after many battles within the Board of Trustees. That change is exemplified by the three women "Global Scholars" who received three of the most prestigious honors in undergraduate science and engineering education: Emily Yedinak (a Fulbright U.S. Student), Katherine Moravec  (a Goldwater Scholar) and Betsy Jones (a Whitaker Fellow). They will be studying at the University of Santiago (Chile), at Harvard and at Oxford, respectively.

James C. Conwell was named president of Rose-Hulman after the unfortunate, sudden, death in April, 2012, of Matt Branan, Rose-Hulman's 14th president. According to Conwell's published pronouncements as he starts out, he will continue the role of the presidents, faculty and administrators who have helped Rose to continue being the number one engineering undergraduate school in the country. Echoes Magazine, the Rose-Hulman publication for alumni, reports on Dr. Conwell's ambitions for Rose-Hulman:

"A top priority…is increasing national and international awareness of Rose-Hulman's reputation as a top undergraduate science, engineering, and mathematics institution…increase the diversity of the student body…better prepare graduates to address global issues by encouraging them to study abroad. "(T)he challenge for us as the leading undergraduate engineering institute in the world is to take this education and teach our students how to do something even more meaningful with it."

Tammy Coons, Executive Assistant to the Board of Trustees, carries on Rose-Hulman's tradition of staff dedication. Among other valuable information on Rose-Hulman's history, she provided the vintage photos at the beginning of chapters three and five.

FELLOW ROSE ALUMNUS AND FRIEND **MIKE PERCOPO**, whom I wrote about earlier, went into the Air Force and spent his time in the Far East, mostly in the Burma area. He spent the rest of his professional life at Squibb, mostly in South America, in Argentina and Brazil. Surprisingly, his first job was an assignment to build a penicillin plant in Turkey. So Mike went off to Turkey and built the plant. He got what was a very good salary at that time. While he had hoped to become president of Squibb itself, he remained president of Squibb International.

Because of his and my international travel responsibilities, Mike and I met a lot of times overseas, often in Tokyo. And whenever I was in New York, Mike and I got together for lunch or dinner.

Mike married a young lady who had worked in the Squibb libraries in New Jersey. She had gone to one of the big, famous women's colleges in the East. They were married for quite a number of years when his wife, unfortunately, died of cancer. Some time after his first wife died, Mike met a lady in New York. She was quite different from his first wife.

Mike lived with this lady for several years until she finally agreed to marry him. They had a few years together in his home in the United Nations Plaza. When they got married, Mike bought another apartment next door, doubling the size of their home. I was quite happy to see them married and his new wife looking after him.

After his retirement, Mike spent most of his time playing the stock market, puts and calls I understand, and was quite successful, as he accumulated several million dollars. After much persuasion from me, Mike left over six million to Rose Poly, and about two million to his first wife's women's college in the East. Mike passed away in January, 2003.

OF ALL THE PEOPLE WHO WORKED for Borg-Warner Chemicals in the Parkersburg, West Virginia plant, there were only a few that I continued to keep in touch with. Or more importantly, who kept in touch with me. Here are three that I still talk to once in awhile.

Roger Chapman now owns a very successful plastic compounding plant in Evansville, Indiana. I visited him on one occasion, probably in the early 2000s. He was very typical of local people we hired at Borg-Warner who were very good workers. Roger was one of the people that the company sent to college, in his case, to Marietta College in Ohio, just across the river, north of Parkersburg, West Virginia.

After quite a few years, Roger left the company, became a

salesman for awhile and ultimately went into business for himself. We still are in touch every few months and he always passes information on to me, either about the people who worked for us who died or about those whose news items became available.

I enjoy my friendship with Roger extremely not only because he is a loyal friend but because he has really made something of himself. From very limited beginnings, he now is a relatively wealthy man. Every time we talk, he still mentions how much he appreciates what Borg-Warner Chemicals did for him.

Through Roger Chapman, I was made aware of an article in a November, 2013, Plastics News publication about the Borg-Warner Chemicals property in Washington, West Virginia, that was originally purchased by Jack Welch of General Electric. It is now destined to become the site of an ethane cracker and three polyethylene plants. Jack Welch's successor finally sold the original Borg-Warner ABS business to Sabic, the big plastics business of Saudi Arabia. Apparently, the very large Brazilian company Braskem SA is the investor of this major petrochemical complex on the approximately 200 acre site which is only a few miles from Parkersburg, West Virginia.

Ted Gateman and his family moved to Parkersburg, West Virginia in 1958. They were neighbors of ours and we got well acquainted right away. Fifty- some years later we are still friends.

Ted is very conservative politically and we don't always see things in the same way, but this has made absolutely no difference in our mutual friendship. As a result of being such close neighbors and my frequent travel to Europe, it seemed quite natural that Ted came with me for his first trip to Europe. Ted traveled with me to Europe many times after that. When we had a few days to spare, I usually knew good places to stay.

To me, Ted is the typical American entrepreneur. He had inherited a small, second-hand lumber business from his father. Starting at that point, Ted began his business by first building natural wooden pallets and then further expanding from there. He eventually got into not only traditional packaging materials, but also into reclaimed packaging for military parts and also for the automotive business. He certainly has built a big commercial business and I have admired him ever since I met him.

Despite the fact that we are close friends, I don't think I would ever want to work for him. He has to have everything under control and is a tough supervisor. Whenever I could, I visited with Ted and his lovely wife Carol and always hope that he comes to Chicago. Unfortunately, I don't get to Parkersburg any more because it's hard to get to Parkersburg from Chicago, but I do talk to him by phone at least every few months. I believe he has sold some of his businesses; meanwhile, he is always working on new ideas and new opportunities. Ted certainly is one of my best and longest-lasting friends.

I ALWAYS HAD SOMEONE HELPING ME as an assistant when I was in the office at Borg-Warner in Parkersburg, West Virginia. I didn't have many assistants, but I did finally attract a good woman secretary and a fellow by the name of **Chuck Padgitt** as my assistant. Chuck did a lot of the functions that I as a manager had to attend to, and I always appreciated his efficiency and effectiveness in carrying out his job.

Chuck is one of the few people from whom I still get birthday cards. In November, 2013, we had our annual telephone conversation. I learned that his wife is recovering from a broken leg, but fortunately she is coming home shortly.

Chuck has been quite a family man. For years he always brought his children together when they were living in the Chicago area. For several decades now Chuck has been residing in Florida, necessary because the humidity is beneficial to him. As of this writing Chuck is now 87 years old and having a very satisfactory life in the eastern Florida area.

Leonard Harvey, a Canadian, was another important fellow and a long-term friend until unfortunately he passed away in 2012. He succeeded me as operations manager and ultimately he ended up in the Chicago Borg-Warner office as executive vice president. He told me a lot about what was going on in the corporate office, much of which we both considered to be not very professional performance.

SOME ADDITIONAL OBSERVATIONS ON PEOPLE. One of my friends picked up a young German girl on the sidewalks of Paris. He took her home, sent her to college, and after graduation, she not only ran his household, but also his office. He got really good service for very little money. Ultimately, he wanted to marry this girl, but he didn't want to use his old political ties to bring her to the USA.

My friend's then-wife, a very nice and handsome lady, suggested that he should divorce her and then bring the girl to this country legitimately. He did just that. His ex-wife then moved to Montreux in Switzerland and had a very satisfactory life in the French Alps with the money she got from the divorce.

One problem that I observed amid quite a number of high level executives: their failure to know how really to handle women. After an executive's wife dies, a lot of those executives were pursued by many women who tried to take advantage of them. Often, that is exactly what happened.

AFTER I RETIRED, OIL COMPANIES in this country had their lawyers look over Borg-Warner Chemicals week after week and month after month.

"Go ahead and buy Borg-Warner Chemicals."

That is what Jack Welch of General Electric (who had always told us how little he thought of us) told his people.

GE acquired our company for much more than they should have paid for it. I saw Jack Welch at the Plastics Show in Chicago a year or so after the purchase in 1988. I asked him why he overpaid so much for the company.

"Oh, we had to have it."

That was his only response.

SOME PARTING THOUGHTS

Chapter 24
Decades, Distances, Discoveries

As I was reviewing all the things I talk about in this book, it occurred to me that there were a lot of lessons I learned along the way that might be helpful to others as well. These lessons are not only from my own experiences, but also from observing others with whom I came in contact. I would like to share some of them with you.

NEW INVENTIONS, PROCESSES. It is instructive to note that most new inventions or processes come from people outside the particular product or industry, because people from the outside don't know what doesn't work. In the case of Borg-Warner, we were told by others what wouldn't work and we were too dumb to know what would work in the polymerization process that made our plastics.

ALLOWING FAILURE. The second consideration is that you have to establish an environment in which people can pursue their own ideas and don't get punished for failures. Bob Shattuck had the unique capability of setting that environment and giving full credit to those who made a new contribution, and he never claimed any of that to himself. Both he and I were very active in recruiting new employees as we rapidly expanded our organization. I probably knew personally about the first 400 people in our organization.

NO PRIMA DONNAS. In looking for new employees, whom we hired primarily from universities and colleges, we always talked to the president of the organization or the institution. In most instances we never hired the top grade graduate, always number 2 or number 3 because number 2 and number 3 were much more likely to fit into an organization that worked together. They were much better in communicating with others, rather than the number 1 who was pretty much always doing things by himself only and not within a group.

It was important for us not to have any prima donnas within the organization and work across disciplines to help each other out, which we did. It so happened that in our case the first contacts with the outside world when we were trying to sell our product was carried out primarily by the research department, the research and development department, so we had very close contacts with our first customers, and that helped greatly in our overall success of the business.

During my working years I ran quite a few times across people, of whom you asked to do something, always came back with the answer "that's not in my job description."

My philosophy always was that when something needed to be done -- and you thought you might be able to do it -- you've just got to go ahead and do it, and the hell with job descriptions. I have absolutely no tolerance for people who can only do what their so-called job descriptions describes. I believe we were so successful because we had people who worked together to get things done and never worried about job descriptions. We didn't need PhDs. We got lab assistants who just came from the country who made very great contributions in developing Cycolac ABS and I believe this was a strong reason for our ultimate success.

TIMING TO MARKET. In bringing your new product to market, it is extremely important not to R&D things forever, but to get the response from potential new consumers as soon as possible because that's the only way to find out whether the product can have commercial success.

Being successful number 1 will usually get you almost 80% of the business and the number 2 will get the other 20% — but only if he can match the number 1's product exactly. A good example is that we invented plating our plastics and when our research people were very hesitant to put it out onto the market because they thought we needed more research work, I told them "It's more important to get it into the hands of potential consumers" which is the only way to find out if something works. So we put it out into the market and kept on working with our potential customers in the final completion of a successful process. The result was that we kept the number 1 position for years, which was very profitable and nobody caught up with us and we had 80% of the market practically from then on in.

ASSESSING NEW PRODUCT SUCCESS POTENTIAL. It is difficult to determine how successful a new product is likely to be and I searched for many years for a good indication of what would make a new product successful.

After talking to probably more than 50 people I got the final answer, for me, from a professor at Rice University in Texas whose name, unfortunately, I don't remember. This professor told me that our product or process is more likely to be successful if it changes any dimension in an exponential way, that is, size, the number of steps, price.

A good example of such exponential changes is the conversion of the vacuum tube to the transistor. Another good example is the Xerox process. The Xerox process was offered to quite a number of companies, including IBM, but they passed it up and it was taken on by Xerox, which was a much smaller company and suffering from financial problems. They made it a success. The other enlightening part of that new copying process was that it was invented not by an engineer but a patent attorney who was looking for a way to make more copies than he could by using carbon copies.

ESTABLISHING/MAINTAINING BUSINESS RELATIONSHIPS. During all my work, whenever I visited chemical companies in this country or anywhere overseas, I made a point of seeing top executives of those companies at least once a year to develop contacts. I always tried to leave some information with them that might be of value, so they would welcome me every future visit. The result of that was licensing the Korea process for additives for PVC which we previously mentioned, and built a very successful business in Europe with a new joint venture plant in Grangemouth, Scotland.

Another good resource for establishing important business relationships is through Board memberships. I talk about a few of the boards I served on and my relationships with people I met on those boards earlier. Serving on external boards is so valuable because you meet new people, get to work closely with them and have many chances to share ideas and contacts among your fellow board members.

RETIRED LIFE. I've never been one to take it easy. The rocking chair was not waiting for me after retiring from my many years at Borg-Warner Chemicals (and I still don't have one). I needed to continue being productive and wanted to share with other businesses what I learned.

I talked about this in the Corporate Life section of this chapter, but I can't emphasize enough the importance of relationships. The many business relationships I maintained over the decades of my employment eventually helped me to establish my own consulting business. It's still global in scope, although I've scaled down much of my international travel.

You've got to cultivate your relationships. Some local people I see as often as once a month. I still keep in contact with others on a regular basis, mostly by phone nowadays, some every couple of months, but at least once a year.

AND FINALLY,

TIMING AND LUCK. I look back in amazement on my modest

beginnings here in the United States. I emigrated from Munich to America in late 1938, barely ahead of Hitler's slaughter of Jews there, and with only $10 in my pocket. Talk about timing!

I talked about the three important pieces of luck that came to me at an early age: getting a four-year scholarship to Rose Poly; meeting Libby, my wife for now 71 years; getting a job at what was to become Borg-Warner Chemicals.

Timing and luck. This country is surely a land of opportunity, as my life in America certainly demonstrates. I hope my story gives everyone who reads this book the desire to become aware of their own instances of timing and luck that are waiting for them, waiting to open wonderful new opportunities.

Some of the greeting cards from my 80th birthday.

HOWARD H. IRVIN

Celebrating Honorary Doctorate from Rose-Hulman

Honorary Degrees

Doctor of Engineering

HOWARD H. IRVIN

Howard H. Irvin graduated from Rose Polytechnic Institute with high honors in 1943. He is also a graduate of the Advanced Management Program of the Harvard Business School.

Mr. Irvin's professional experience includes thirty-eight years with Borg-Warner Corporation, where he held several senior management positions. While at Borg-Warner, Mr. Irvin led the development effort which resulted in Borg-Warner Chemicals being the largest ABS polymer producer in the world. Since 1982, Mr. Irvin has been the President of Howard H. Irvin Associates, a world-wide business consulting firm serving multinational clients with business strategies and technology transfer. In addition, he is a director of Intercorp, Ltd., a London-based firm that emphasizes technical and business cooperation between businesses in the United States, the United Kingdom, and Japan.

Mr. Irvin belongs to the American Chemical Society, Society of Chemical Industry (London), Society of the Plastics Industry, the Licensing Executives Society, and the Harvard Business School Club of Chicago. He is a member of the Rose-Hulman Institute of Technology Board of Managers.

DEPARTMENT OF THE ARMY
UNITED STATES ARMY ROTC BATTALION
ROSE-HULMAN INSTITUTE OF TECHNOLOGY
"WABASH BATTALION"
TERRE HAUTE, INDIANA 47803-3999

REPLY TO
ATTENTION OF:

May 28, 1987

Office of the
Battalion Commander

Mr. Howard H. Irvin
President, Howard H. Irvin Associates
150 N. Michigan Avenue, Suite 2120
Chicago, IL 60601

Dear Mr. Howard:

    I want to thank you for being our guest speaker at the Army ROTC Commissioning Ceremony at Rose-Hulman. Your splendid speech provided our newly commissioned officers with the appropriate words of advise, encouragement, and challenge. I appreciate very much your contribution to this ceremony.

    I also want to congratulate you on receiving an Honorary Doctorate Degree from Rose-Hulman. It is a well-deserved recognition of your excellent accomplishments and leadership. Congratulations!

    The very best of regards to you and Mrs. Irvin.

George
George B. Shoener
Lieutenant Colonel, U.S. Army
Commanding

Copy Furnished:

Dr. Hulbert

THE WHITE HOUSE
WASHINGTON

July 25, 1997

Mr. Howard H. Irvin
Howard H. Irvin Associates
Suite 2910
150 North Michigan Avenue
Chicago, Illinois 60601

Dear Howard:

    Thank you very much for writing to me. It is important to me to hear the views and concerns of people around the country, and I appreciate your taking the time to write. I will certainly keep your thoughts in mind as my Administration continues working to address the challenges our nation faces as we approach the 21st century.

    I hope you will remain involved.

Sincerely,

Bill Clinton

People, Places and Tough Plastics / 159

To Mr. Howard Irvin,
Thank you for the dedication and support you have offered to me, my family, and the Party during the eight years of my administration. You are a true friend.

Bill Clinton

APPENDIX

CHINA, 1974

The following two reports on China are reproduced pretty much as I wrote them in 1974, mostly as a diary to record my own memories. The names of Chinese cities and other areas appear as they were in common use at that time. I think they capture the events much more accurately than if I tried to recall the details of this trip now, in the latter part of 2013. In addition to the Fair, we were able to visit a manufacturing commune (second report).

Canton Fair, 1974

In early September of this year, our company received three invitations for the Fall 1974 Canton Fair from the Chinese government office for promotion of international trade and I was fortunate enough to be able to represent our Chemicals group on this visit. Libby was elated to find that she could get a visa, too, and we were pleased that our visas were obtained very quickly through the Chinese liaison office in Washington.

We left Chicago on the 29th of October for San Francisco, where we stayed overnight. On the next day, we flew non-stop to Tokyo which, because of unfavorable winds, took us 11 1/2 hours, after which we sat around in the Tokyo airport for two more hours and then completed the flight to Hong Kong four hours after that. It was a long flight, rather uneventful, except that we met a couple, both in their 30's, from New York on the Tokyo-Hong Kong leg of our journey.

We found out that the husband had made a million dollars in selling all kinds of junk in several boardwalk stores in Atlantic City. The money, he told us, he had promptly lost, but he was now back working on his next few million dollars. He was going to Hong Kong to check on some of his suppliers of electronic parts which he was having made in Hong Kong for sale in the United States. He was into all kinds of things besides the electronics business and was working on his goal of leaving each one of his five children a million dollars.

I won't go into Libby's psychoanalyzing him; by the time we arrived in Hong Kong, they did agree on what turned him on. One of his new projects was for Evel Knievel to embark on a new feat, namely jumping over Mt. Fuji. By the time I heard that, I wasn't sure how much this guy was leading us on. When I was later in Japan and was in a conversation with several conservative businessmen, I heard reference to this particular venture and it appeared that it was really being planned. If you know anything about the revered position that Mt. Fuji assumes in Japanese cultural and religious life, you will also appreciate how well that one is going to go over with the traditionalists in Japan.

We arrived in Hong Kong about 11:00 at night, Hong Kong time. Hong Kong airport, which is always a madhouse, was only more so because the previous day a typhoon had hit Hong Kong (unusual for that time of the year) and no flights had gone in or out. Many stranded passengers were still coming in and we were caught up in all of that.

In Hong Kong, we met with two other representatives of our company who were also going to the Fair. We also met the president and vice president of the Chicago Association of Commerce and Industry and their wives, who had also been invited to the Fair.

The next two days were spent on various briefings and meetings with people in Hong Kong, partly with Americans who had previously gone to the Fair, with representatives of the liaison office of the Peoples' Republic of China, and many other "old hands" on China who helped me to get a better understanding of what to expect.

Libby managed to go shopping here and there. Prices in Hong Kong have gone sky high and knowing my wife, you should appreciate that she is always out bargain-hunting. On Sunday, I accompanied her to Cat Street which is an area with lots of stands where such "bargains" can be found.

About 8:30 in the morning on November 4, we set out for our trip to Canton, having on the previous Saturday gotten tickets for our trip from the China Travel Service, which is the Peoples' Republic travel office in Hong Kong which makes all the arrangements for travel and hotel.

Having gotten our visas in the United States, the formalities for getting the tickets were dispensed with efficiently and quickly; for the Hong Kong equivalent of about $45.00 (U.S.) each, we got tickets for a first class, round trip to Canton and a meal ticket for lunch on the trip out.

The trip from Hong Kong to the border took about two hours. It was a slow journey with many stops. The train was crowded, the weather was rainy and messy, but, of course, everybody was greatly anticipating this new adventure.

When we got off the train at Shun Chun, we first had to go through Hong Kong immigration and then walked to the now famous railroad bridge that all of you have seen in pictures, where uniformed Chinese border officials took our passports and waived us across the bridge into a building where we waited for processing. It is no longer necessary to lug your own luggage across the bridge. This is now all taken care of for the traveler.

There were a fair number of Americans, but many French, some Italians, a few Swiss, and a few Scandinavians in the area where we were waiting to get our passports back. The many Japanese on the train waited in a separate area and we also saw no visitors from either eastern Europe or Africa who, likewise, were apparently processed separately, although there weren't very many in evidence. After about a half hour or so of waiting, the same officials came back with stacks of passports shouting out the names, but obviously with problems in pronouncing them properly. Eventually, everyone had their passports back.

Customs was no problem. While we had to list radios or jewelry or money or photographic equipment, everything went very smoothly without much delay and less of a hassle than we would experience in returning to Honolulu, for instance.

After customs clearance, we went to a large waiting room with soft chairs and drank tea while waiting for lunch to be served. When lunch was served, it was good and adequate, but some veterans bitched that they usually served fruit which was not forthcoming, apparently a logistics problem that day. Since our B-W contingent was not in the first rush to get to the tables, we all ended up scattered at different tables. I sat next to a young Swiss who had been coming for five years to buy vegetable oils.

After lunch, we boarded the train for Canton; it was very clean, excellently equipped, and provided a smooth ride through the countryside. We were offered hot tea, assuming it was complementary, but later found out that they collected per cup. Since we didn't have any change, we ended up getting it free anyway.

Dollar traveler checks were easily exchanged at the border for Ren Min Bin, equal to about 50 U.S. cents each. The trip through the countryside was very interesting. The fields are relatively small, most all areas are cultivated with rice; there is a great deal of water visible, and lots of ducks populate that water. Ducks appeared to be very precious to the Chinese. We almost didn't have the heart to eat one - but they are very tasty.

We saw people working in the fields or on the roads as we looked out the train window, but not too many. Some were riding bicycles or carrying various items. Thinking of 700-900 million people, seeing so few was unexpected. We saw some men who had made rain capes out of leaves or straw that looked very unusual.

We got to Canton after about 1 1/2 hours by about 3:00 in the afternoon. When we got off, we entered a brand new railroad station which was huge, roomy, and clean. We rode an escalator from track to street level where we got on small busses that took us to the Tung Fong Hotel where all Westerners are quartered; this was about ten minutes from the station and right across from the new Fair building.

The Tung Fong Hotel looked like it was built perhaps in the late 1920s with high ceilinged rooms and old-fashioned furniture, but it was, nevertheless, quite adequate and comfortable with elevator service. A new wing was recently built which is more modern, with rooms smaller and ceilings lower, but well constructed.

Our hotel room was quite comfortable. The young men and women assigned to each floor to handle laundry and services lived in small, crowded dormitory rooms on each floor. The hotel had good facilities for banking, for sending cables, for buying books, other literature, stamps and foodstuffs, and souvenirs. On one floor of the hotel were the offices for the Trade Fair, where we registered.

We were received by very friendly English speaking personnel who appeared to be quite young. Through them, we were able to make arrangements for meeting the various trading organizations that we wanted to see.

The traffic at the Fair was not all that great this year, so it was not too difficult to arrange appointments fairly readily. On another floor of the hotel was an office of the China Travel Service where we had to leave our passports for the local registration; every time anyone wanted to go on an excursion, his passport had to be validated for visits away from Canton, so the movements of all foreigners are quite effectively controlled, but one never feels under particular pressure of being spied on or watched. I believe the locals are also required to obtain travel permits.

We were surprised to find how well the people who were assigned to help the visitors spoke English, and found out that most of them were university students who had been brought from Peking or Shang-Hai for the duration of the Fair to practice their English. English, French, German and Spanish were spoken by these interpreters. However, it appeared that each one could manage only one language.

A new Fair building with many permanent exhibitions was inaugurated at the Spring Fair this year, and the buildings and displays were quite well done. For those who were not tied up with the Fair, various visits could be arranged to communes, to schools, to some factories, and for general sight-seeing in and around Canton.

What impresses one most in coming to a place like Canton, which is a city of about two million people, is that one doesn't see any of the abject poverty as in India, for instance. Everyone seems to be well fed and adequately clothed. The children are just like children anywhere and they seemed well taken care of and happy. They are also much more colorful, because their clothing is not the stereotype clothing that the adults wear.

Pants and Mao jackets are still the attire that everybody wears, although the young girls are beginning to wear blouses of different colors, and I noticed that many of the men at the Fair wore regular short or long sleeved white shirts with gray trousers. While you don't see any jewelry displayed by anyone, quite a few of the people we saw had at least wrist watches.

While it is true that everybody is dressed the same, depending on your position in the hierarchy, you may have a jacket or pants that fit better, are made of better cloth, and for some of the higher officialdom, probably custom tailored clothing, and I don't mean by Hong Kong tailors. The fact that everyone wears the same clothes tends not to bother you after you're there for a while and you almost forget about it.

Canton is probably one of the most open cities in China and may have almost more foreign visitors than any other place in China at present, yet whenever foreigners are standing or walking somewhere, people do collect and watch because foreign visitors in all their finery are still a rare sight.

We were most impressed by the friendliness of all the people whom we came in contact with, although we were told that the atmosphere in the South is much freer than it is up north in Peking; no different than in any other country in the world. People in the South are a lot more easy-going, and more jovial than the people in the North.

I did talk to some of the commercial attaches who are stationed in Peking: Dutch, Australians, Canadians and a Finnish couple. They told me that life in Peking is a lot more grim, and that their contact with officialdom is a lot more restricted than it is at the Fair. In fact, their contact with the Chinese is quite limited, and waiting for official appointments is frustrating.

We had been told that food is excellent in Canton. Since we made some good Chinese friends among the visitors, primarily from Hong Kong, we were able to get an outstanding introduction to good Chinese fare. There are some expensive restaurants that prepare special meals which cost on the order of between $7.00 and $10.00 a person, where perhaps up to 12 courses might be served, but one night I took eight people to dinner at our hotel, where I had previously been warned that the prices were quite high; although no one ate very luxuriously, we all had an excellent meal and the total bill came to only $13.00. The double room in the hotel was $12.00 a night, so you can see that Canton takes less advantage of its Fair visitors than any major western city.

The Chinese pride themselves on the fact that they have had very little inflation and that their prices have been stable internally since the late 1940s. I did point out to them that this was not necessarily true for the goods that they were selling at the Fair, and to that I didn't get a very good answer. We did visit their friendship store which is a department store that offers wares for sale; we didn't see anything exciting there, except for Mao jackets and caps, very well made and of good quality for about $4.00 each. There was one antique store in Kwangchow where one can buy things that are up to maybe 200 years old, authenticated, and which are permitted to be taken out of the country. Antiques export is tightly controlled and one needs special permission for each item. We did like and acquire a few small vases, a teapot and some ivory chop sticks that had been sheathed in silver.

There are many large parks in Canton, Despite the fact that the housing in the city is quite crowded and fairly decrepit, the parks make it very nice. Our guides also prided themselves on the fact that they had moved many of the people who had been living on boats on the Pearl River into apartment buildings they have put up. I wasn't sure whether the people who had had a certain amount of privacy on these boats and are now in cramped quarters in apartments necessarily felt that this was an improvement.

The propaganda we were exposed to was fairly subtle and subdued compared to what people had to endure at some of the early fairs. Going back five or ten years or so, they had, in most cases, listened to maybe a half hour of indoctrination before finally starting to talk business. This was not at all the case at this time and the slogans we saw on the various banners around the Fair and the city were some that I think most of us could subscribe to, exhorting people to work hard to build the country and to contribute to everyone's welfare.

Incidentally, some of the merchandise and the machinery we saw at the Fair looked quite good to me. Many of the people I talked to thought the Chinese were way behind times, and that some of the machinery was maybe 30 or 40 years behind our own developments. I believe what people overlook is the fact that what is needed there, and what we need, are two different things; rugged equipment requiring little maintenance is what is most useful in that part of the world.

On the last of our five days in Canton, we were able to visit part of a commune of considerable size, consisting of about 20,000 people, which I write about below (Shahsi Production Brigade). This included a boat trip up the Pearl River, one of the major waterways in China and on the banks of which Canton is located.

We were told that this was the first time they had authorized a boat trip. Major ocean going vessels can come up the river all the way to Canton and I understand that in 1975, one of the major cruise vessels will actually dock in Canton. The trip up the river was about two and one half hours long. It was, of course, interesting to not only watch the river traffic, but also to see some of the facilities that had been built up along the shore.

We went by a naval shipyard where they were building vessels which seemed to be of a size up to perhaps 20,000 ton capacity; missile launchers were visible on several of them. They were also building some tankers and some smaller escort vessels.

While much can be said for the medical treatment in China, it may still be quite primitive. Nevertheless, their acupuncture methods have certainly caught the imagination of every country in the world; in some things, they may be way behind, but in other ways, they are also ahead. The fact that they have managed to feed a population of 800 to 900 million people where they used to have famines that killed millions and millions is an accomplishment any country can be proud of. If we can believe what we are told, there is no use of dope, there is no venereal disease in China, practically no crime, and above all, no tipping. The people we were able to see and came in contact with seemed to be quite happy and content; certainly their material needs are very, very modest.

After the boat trip, we arrived at the commune where we visited one brigade (the brigade is a sub-division). It was a farming community, as we might have seen in this country or in Europe 40 or 50 years ago, perhaps a bit more primitive. The brigade had their own school, a machine shop, brewery, implements of mechanization, and a rather crude hospital and maternity ward, but at least it appeared that the people were able to eke out an acceptable living, but without any luxuries.

Everybody works and gets paid -- if you don't work, you don't get paid, and if you are sick and have to go to the hospital or have any kind of treatment, you pay half of the charge for that yourself. So that helps to get people to work and at the same time, keeps them from being sick when they really don't have any ailments. That should be something for us to think about in this "capitalistic" welfare society of ours; we make a lot of money available for people when they don't work or when they pretend to be sick. In their society, this does not happen.

The fields we saw were relatively small and, therefore, impossible to cultivate by modern mass production agricultural methods. They fed us an excellent lunch of five or six courses; the food was very good and appeared to be plentiful. Incidentally, we were quite amazed at how many of the Chinese were eating in the various restaurants in Canton. This must indicate that food is essentially very cheap and that because of the crowded quarters in which they live, the people try to take every opportunity they have to eat out.

We probably could go on and on in telling you about our visit. All I can say is that all the Westerners we were with were impressed with what they saw: a society which seemed to be functioning quite well and in which people appeared to be reasonably happy with their lot.

All of us would have liked to go beyond Canton, but it is practically impossible to do so without a special permit, and it will take another year or so before they have more facilities to accommodate tourist travel. I am quite confident though that it will come, and that the country will become more open to foreigners.

There is, of course, a big debate going on as to what will happen when Chou En-lai and Mao fade out of the picture. The general consensus is that no one individual will emerge as the leader because the Chinese are trying to avoid any one individual becoming dominant, with the exception that Mao is still a revered leader of his country.

Mao, incidentally, started the revolution in Canton where he had a compound of various buildings in which cadres of young, bright people were trained for a period of six months in Marxist ideology military discipline and tactics. These were then sent back into the country to stir up the peasants into a revolt. Over a period of a few years, they probably trained five or six hundred people who became the nucleus of the Mao-ist movement. This complex of buildings is still in tact. The movement apparently operated right under the noses of the then existing political hierarchy.

At the end of the sixth day, we arrived back in Hong Kong - having had an experience which no more than two years ago we would have thought of as just an idle dream.

P.S. I didn't want to bore you with the business aspects, but I neither sold nor bought very much on this trip!

Shahsi Production Brigade, Panyu County

The Shahsi Production Brigade of the Tashih Commune, Panyu County, has 18 production teams, 705 families and over 2,900 people. Its total cultivated land is 3,003 mou (200 hectares). of which 2,657 mu (177 hectares) are paddy fields and 205 mu (13 odd hectares) are orchards.

"Water conservation is the life-blood of agriculture."

Following Chairman Mao's instruction, the brigade has carried out farm capital construction and water conservancy projects in a big way. It has successively strengthened 11 kilometer stone (stone-faced) dykes, built 15 big and small sluice gates and installed across its fields a network of low voltage power lines, 11 kilometers in all.

It has also purchased 3 tractors, 108 threshers and over 400 boats of different sizes as well as diesel engines, generators, motor boats, electric sprinklers and insecticide sprayers. In addition, it runs a foundry, a brewery and enterprises like ship repairing, grain processing, paint spraying, straw- bale manufacturing and cement-bag making.

With its own investment, the brigade is now moving the embankments outwards to reclaim 1,090 mou (72.3 hectares) of farmland, thereby expanding its present acreage by 40%.

In 1956, during the high tide of agricultural collectivization, the output of rice in this brigade averaged 1,000 catties (a cattie is about 1.5 lbs or 680 grams) a mou. In the early years after communization the record figure was 1,200 catties. And since the Great Proletarian Cultural Revolution it has risen to well over 1,500 catties. Of the 14 rice crops harvested from 1966 to 1972, 9 have topped the targets set in the National Programme for Agricultural Development. In recent years the total annual yield of rice has exceeded 4 million catties, one million catties higher than 1963, the year before the movement of "Learning from Tachi in agriculture" was unfolded.

The brigade has at the same time made use of the dykes, the waste plots and all the scraps of land by the roadside, at the backyard, etc. and planted 3,200 bamboos and 23,300 fruit trees, such as lichee, pomegranate, mango, jack fruit, loquat, lemon, plum, pomelo, papaya, mandarin and palm. Now both sides of its 11 kilometer dykes are lined with fruit trees and bamboo groves. This has not only provided beautiful landscapes but also added to its collective income.

Its diversified economy has made considerable headway too. The total income in 1972 was 11 million yuan, half of which came from its diversified economy. With the development of its production, the income of the members has also increased year after year. In 1972 the average income per capita was 222 yuan, as against 186 yuan in 1971, registering an increase of 36 yuan. (200 Yuan = $100 U.S.)

CHAPTER NOTES

FOREWARD
Launch of Chicago High Tech Association:
http://news.medill.northwestern.edu/assets/0/18/20/74/76/f7e79327482c4cf68867bc31e03893ef.swf

CHAPTER 5
Jews in America make up 2.2% of the population
http://www.jewishvirtuallibrary.org/jsource/US-Israel/usjewpop.html

22% of Nobel Prize winners worldwide are Jews:
http://www.jinfo.org/Nobel_Prizes.html

CHAPTER 10
http://www.hotrod.com/features/history/articles/0501kc-history-of-piranha-kit-cars/

http://www.forgottenfiberglass.com/fiberglass-car-marques/crvmarbonpiranhaseagull/introducing-the-crv-cycolac-research-vehicle-by-marbon-chemicals-1965/

CHAPTER 14
The Making of Scotland: A Comprehensive Guide to the Growth of its Cities, Towns, and Villages by John R. Hume, Robin Smith and Alan Lawson (Nov 20, 2002)
Grangemouth, Scotland to build plant

CHAPTER 17
The Design World of Micky Nakayasu (July, 1998) appears to be only available in Japan: http://www.amazon.co.jp/The-design-world-Micky-Nakayasu

CHAPTER 20
A Man of Vision: The Story of Paul Pinsky
http://www.amazon.com/Man-Of-Vision-Story-Pinsky/dp/B0006RONHI

CHAPTER 21
Joel Hochberg, the Docmeister, lists his favorite video documentaries at
http://www.youtube.com/playlist?list=PL968C1608630415C5

CHAPTER 22
http://www.rose-hulman.edu/news/on-campus/2012/rose-hulman-gets-all-time-best-score-to-top-national-undergraduate-engineering-rankings.aspx

http://www.rose-hulman.edu/news/on-campus/2012/rose-hulman-saddened-by-loss-of-president-matt-branam.aspx

At Any Cost: Jack Welch, General Electric, and the Pursuit of Profit By Thomas F. O'Boyle, Jan. 2011:
http://www.randomhouse.com/book/123102/at-any-cost-by-thomas-f-oboyle/9780307773234/

INDEX

A

Abbott Laboratories, 81
ABS plastics, ii, ix, 46-47, 49-52, 54, 56, 67-69, 77, 82, 92, 146, 152
Acapulco, Mexico, 132
Adhesives, 42-45, 51
AFL-CIO, 122
Algiers, Algeria, 120
Alps
    Bavarian, 18
    French, 109
    Swiss, 109
Amsterdam, Netherlands, 74-75, 104
Argentina, 129-130, 132
Art, ix, 16, 92, 100-101, 118, 119, 121, 130, 131
Arthur D. Little, 87-88
AT&T, ii, 49-50, 67
Australia, 14, 76-77, 92
    Melbourne, 76
Automotive industry, 29-30, 43, 52, 69

B

Bakelite, 49
Baker, George, 61
Bangkok, Thailand, 92-93
Bank of Scotland, 70
Barcelona, Spain, 116
Barry, George, 56
Baur au Lach Hotel, Switzerland, 109
Bavaria, Germany, 18, 105-106
Belgium, 75, 118
    Brussels, 74-75, 118-119
Bell Labs, 49-50
Beré, James F. (Jim), ii, 64, 81-83
Bibendum Restaurant, U.K., 114
Black Forest Region, Germany, 105
Blendex, 68-70
Bloomberg, Ben Family, 25, 33
Bodenbach, Czech Republic, 13-14
Borg, George, 41
Borg-Warner, ii, 39-42, 56-57, 59, 64-67, 72-73, 75-81, 84, 87, 92, 96, 98, 116, 130, 135, 139, 147
Borg-Warner Chemicals, 54, 56, 69, 75, 83, 88, 103-104, 118, 145-148
Boston Consulting, 88
Braskem SA, 146
Brazil, 77, 129
    Copa Cabana, 129
    Rio de Janeiro, 129
    Sao Paulo, 77
British Petroleum, 69
Brown, Milton, 61
Brussels, Belgium, 74-75, 118-119
Burkeville, Virginia, 23-24

C

Cairo, Egypt, 124-125
Calvert, Bill, 53, 79
Canada, 76, 114
    Cobourg, 76
    Lake Ontario, 76
Canton Fair: 1974, 76, 162-171
Chamberlain, Neville (Former British Prime Minister), 21
Charlton, Bobby, 128-129
Chapman, Roger, 145-146
Cheese, 102, 110-111, 113, 115
Chesterfield Hotel, London, 114
Chicago, 64, 133-135
Chicago, University of, 80
China, People's Republic of
    Canton (now Guangzhou) 162-171
    Panyu County (now a Guangzhou district), 171-172
    Shanghai, 90-92
Churchill, Winston, 121
Cobourg, Lake Ontario, Canada, 76
Cohn, Dr. James H., 138
Coimbra, Portugal, 117
Conrad Hotel, England, 114
Conwell, James C. 144
Coons, Tammy, 144
Copacabana, Brazil, 129
Copenhagen, Denmark, 103-104
Cordoba, Spain, 117
Costa del Sol, Spain, 116-117
Cotswalds, U.K., 114

Cyclized natural rubber, 41-42, 44-45
Cycolac ABS, 45-47, 49-51, 54, 56, 67-69, 77, 82, 132
Czech Republic, 13-14
    Bodenbach, 13-14

D

Delfín, Victor, 100, 130
Dempsey, Jerry E., 77, 135
Denmark, 103
    Copenhagen, 103-104
Der Käfer restaurant, Munich, 106
Dordogne area, France, 112
Drizin, Jeff, 136-137
duPont de Nemours and Company, E. I., 47, 55, 58-59

E

Edinburgh, Scotland, U.K., 114
Egypt, 1240125
Emanuel, Rahm (Mayor of Chicago) 134

F

Farmer, Tom
Feder, Dr. Robert, 138-139
Fez, Morocco, 120-121
Ford, Edsel, 30-31
Ford, Henry, 29-31
Ford Motor Corporation, 29-31, 56
Formentor Hotel, Majorca, 117-118
Four Seasons Hotel, Munich, 105
France, 57, 62, 68-69, 102-103, 112-113, 116
    Dordogne area, 112
    French Riviera, 113
    Nice, 62, 113
    Paris, 62, 69, 112-113, 115-116
    Versailles, 112
Franziskaner Restaurant, Munich, 106

French Alps, 109
Friedman, Elliott, 139

G

Gardner, Ava, 117
Gary, Indiana, 39-42, 45, 53, 59
Gateman, Ted, 146-147
Gay Hussar, The, (Hungarian Restaurant, London) 114-115
Geismar, Louisiana, 48
General Electric, 56, 146, 148
Genoa, Italy, 110-111
Germany
    Bavaria, 18, 105-106
    Black Forest Region, 105
    Munich, 14-16, 18, 22, 97, 101, 105-106, 142-143, 155
    Stuttgart, 14, 106-107
Gilbert, Ms., 24
Gill, Dr. Manjot, 139
Givat Haviva, 121, 123, 125-126
Goodyear Tire Company, 42, 79
Gothenburg, Sweden, 104
Grangemouth, Scotland, 70

H

Haifa Institute of Technology, 58
Harrods Department Store, 115
Harvard Business School, 60-63
Harvey, Leonard, 147
Hawaii, 121-123
Hong Kong, 58, 91, 93-96, 162-164, 167
Hilton Hotel, Shanghai, 91
Hitler, Adolph, ii, 15, 21, 32, 155
Hochberg, Joel and Barbara, 137
Hokkaido, Japan, 97
Hotel Cambon, Paris, 112
Hotel Majestic, Rome, 111
Hotel Splendido, Portofino, 111

I

ICI (Imperial Chemical Industries), 68
IMD Business School, 62-63
Imperial Hotel, Japan, 97
Indiana
    Gary, 39-42, 45, 53, 59
    Indianapolis, 24, 50, 143
    Terre Haute, 23-26, 33
Ingersoll, Robert (Bob), 73, 75-76
Inland Steel, 33, 39-40
Interlaken, Switzerland, 109
Irvin, Libby (nee Tarler), I, ii, 33-35, 63, 66, 74, 93, 98, 101, 109, 116, 118, 121, 124-125, 129, 132-133, 138, 140, 155, 162-163
Irvin, Robert, 34-35
Israel, 123-125
    Haifa, 58
    Tel Aviv, 125
Italian Riviera, 113
Italy
    Genoa, 110-111
    Lake Como, 110
    Lake Garda, 110
    Milan, 110-111
    Portofino, 110-111
    Rome, 111

J

Jamaica
    Kingston, 128
    Lucea, 127
    Montego Bay, 127
Japan
    Hokkaido, 97
    Kyushu, 71, 73, 97
    Sapporo, 97
    Tokyo, 68, 71, 73, 94, 96-98
    Ube City, 71-72, 90, 96-98
Japanese Americans, 59

K

Kaiser, Tom, 80-82

Kaufman, Al, 56-58
Kibbutzim, 126
Kingston, Jamaica, 128
Kissinger, Henry, 66, 75, 136
Kolb, Fred, 27-28
Kulm Hotel, Switzerland, 109
Kureha Chemical Company, Japan, 68-69, 96
Kyushu, Japan, 71, 73, 97

L

Lake Como, Italy, 110
Lake Garda, Italy, 110
Lake Geneva, Switzerland, 109
Lake Ontario, Canada, 76
Lausanne, Switzerland, 62, 109
Lego (The Lego Group), 103
Lima, Peru, 130-131
Linderhof Castle, Munich, 106
Lisbon, Portugal, 117
London, U.K., 14-15, 21, 74, 113-115
Louisiana, 47-48
Lucea, Jamaica, 127

M

Machu Picchu, Peru, 130-131
Madrid, Spain, 116
Majorca, 117-118
Molter, Ernst, 107-108
Marrakech, Morocco, 121
Mamounia Hotel, Marrakech, 121
Mandarin Oriental Hotel, Munich, 105
Marbon Chemicals, 39-42, 44, 53, 62, 79, 82, 83
Marbon S, 42, 44
McCurry, Bill, 79
Melbourne, Australia, 76
Merrill Lynch, 82, 87
Mexico
    Acapulco, 132
    Mexico City, 131
Michel, Jim, Sr. and Jr., 139-140
Midlands, U.K., 68-69

Milan, Italy, 110-111
Miner, Tom, 135-136
Mitsukoshi, Department Store,
    Japan, 94
Model A Ford, 28, 30-31
Monsanto, 53, 55, 58
Montego Bay, Jamaica, 127
Morelli, Mike, 140
Morocco, Africa
    Fez, 120-121
    Marrakech, 121
    Rabat, 120
Munich, Germany, 14-16, 18, 22, 97,
    101, 105-106, 142-143, 155

N

Nakayasu, Kenichi, 71-72
Nakayasu, Micky, 98-99
Netherlands
    Amsterdam, 74-75, 104
Nice, France, 62, 113
Northwestern Memorial Hospital
    138-139
Northwestern University, 33
Norway
    Oslo, 104
Nylex Company, 76-77
Nylon, 51, 71, 82

O

Oslo, Norway, 104

P

Padgitt, Chuck, 147
Paris, France, 62, 69, 112-113,
    115-116
Parkersburg, West Virginia, 47-48,
    53, 78, 145-147
Parsons, Russell, 83
Patents, 44-45, 51, 79
Patton, George, 57
Peninsula Hotel, Chicago, 134
Peninsula Hotel, Hong Kong, 95

People's Republic of China, 75-76,
    90-91, 96, 162-172
Percopo, Mike, 24-25, 62, 143-145
Peru
    Lima, 130-131
    Machu Picchu, 130-131
Pinsky, Paul, 121-123
Polycarbonate, 50-51
Polyvinyl, 41-42, 68
Portofino, Italy, 110-111
Portugal
    Coimbra, 117
    Lisbon, 117
PVC, 68, 154

R

Rabat, Morocco, 120
Ragle, Jack, 26, 143
RCA, 46-47, 50, 52
Reagan, President Ronald, 136
Renault vehicles, 69
Richmond, Virginia, 22-24
Ritz Hotel, Lisbon, 117
Rio de Janeiro, Brazil, 130
Rome, Italy, 111
Rose-Hulman (formerly Rose
    Polytechnic Institute), 23, 24-28
    39, 58-59, 63, 143-145, 155-156
Russell, Sam, 45-46, 52-53, 70, 74

S

Sabic, (Saudi Basic Industries
    Corporation), 146
Sao Paulo, Brazil, 77
Sadat, Anwar, daughter of, 124-126
Sapporo, Japan, 97
Sapporo Beer, 97
SBR (synthetic rubber), 42
Schwabing, Munich, Germany. 16
Scotland, 68-70, 74, 113-114, 154
    Edinburg, 114
    Grangemouth, 70
Sea Island Hotel, Lucea, Jamaica,
    127

Selfridges, London, 115
Selz, Peter, 22
Seville, Spain, 117
Shanghai, China, People's Republic of, 90-92
Shattuck, Robert, 39-40, 44, 45, 47, 49, 58-59, 67, 71-72, 79-81, 135, 143, 151
Spain
    Barcelona, 116
    Cordoba, 117
    Costa del Sol, 116-117
    Madrid, 116
    Seville, 117
Spainhour, Jim, 58, 81, 92
Springborn, Robert, 58
St. Gallen, Switzerland, 109
St. Moritz, Switzerland, 108-110
Stanford, Rosalie, 140-141
Stratford, , U.K., 114
Strauss, Isidore, 61
Stuttgart, Germany, 14, 106-107
Styrene, 42, 44-47, 50, 55, 70
Suiter, Bill, 83
Sweden, 104-105
    Gothenburg, 104
Switzerland
    Interlaken, 109
    Lausanne, 62, 109
    Lake Geneva, 109
    St. Gallen, 109
    St. Moritz, 108-110
    Swiss Alps, 109
    Zermatt, 57-58
    Zurich, 109

T

Taita Chemical Company, 92
Taiwan
    Taipei, 92
Tarler (Irvin) Libby, ii, 33
Tau Beta Pi (engineering society), 27
Tel Aviv, Israel, 125
Telephone housings, 49-50
Terre Haute, Indiana, 23-26, 33
Thailand
    Bangkok, 92-93
Thalheimer, Bill, 22
Tokyo, Japan, 68, 71, 73, 94, 96-98
TWA, 78

U

Ube, Japan, 71-72, 90, 96-98
Ube Cycon, 72, 90
Ube Industries, , 71, 98
Ube Kosan, 97
Union Carbide, 55
Unions, 54, 59, 122
Uniroyal, div. U.S. Rubber, 44-46
United Kingdom
    Cotswolds, 114
    Edinburg, Scotland, 114
    London, 14-15, 21, 74, 113-115
    Stratford

V

Villa d'Este, Italy, 110
Virginia, 22-24
    Burkeville, 23-24
Vitamin D, 80-82
Volker, Paul, 136

W

Warburg, Ingrid, 22
Welch, Jack, 146, 148
Wells Fargo Advisory Services, 139
West Virginia, 47-48, 53, 55-56, 58, 64, 133, 145-147
Whitechapel, London, 21
Willersinn, Dr. Herbert, 82
Wolseley Piccadilly Restaurant, London, 114

Z

Zermatt, Switzerland, 57-58
Zurich, Switzerland, 109

www.ingramcontent.com/pod-product-compliance
Lightning Source LLC
Chambersburg PA
CBHW041509220426
43661CB00047B/1515